FACE *to* FACE

SEEKING A PERSONAL
RELATIONSHIP WITH GOD

S. MICHAEL WILCOX

DESERET
BOOK

Salt Lake City, Utah

For Laurie, my Rachel, as part of the seven years

Visit us at DeseretBook.com

Library of Congress Cataloging-in-Publication Data

Wilcox, S. Michael, author.
  Face to face : seeking a personal relationship with God / S. Michael Wilcox.
      pages cm
  Includes bibliographical references and index.
    ISBN 978-1-60907-520-0 (hardbound : alk. paper)
    1. Mormons—Conduct of life. 2. Prayer—The Church of Jesus Christ of Latter-day Saints. 3. Revelation—The Church of Jesus Christ of Latter-day Saints. I. Title.
    BX8635.3.W53 2013
    248.4'89332—dc23   2013014166

Printed in the United States of America
R. R. Donnelley, Crawfordsville, IN

10   9   8   7   6   5   4   3   2   1

Contents

THAT THEY SHOULD SEEK THE LORD,
if haply they might feel after him, and find him,
though he be not far from every one of us: for in
him we live, and move, and have our being.

—ACTS 17:27—28

FACE TO FACE

Lord, teach us to pray,
as John also taught his disciples.

—Luke 11:1

CEILINGS

When I was a child, my mother taught me to pray. As all children do, I knelt down and followed the formula my mother gave me—we thanked, we asked, we blessed. At first she said the words and I repeated them, but as I grew older, I could talk to my Father in Heaven on my own. A child's mind comes up with some of the most interesting thoughts and questions. Many are simply delightful and others are of such complexity that even the most mature and intelligent don't have a good answer. My question as a child was really very simple. I recall kneeling alone in my room and looking up at the ceiling and wondering how my words could get through. My concept of God was that he was "up," rather than around me or by my side, and all that ceiling overhead was surely a barrier. How could my words reach him? I was down here and he lived in the sky somewhere above the roof. I pictured my prayers as almost physical things, pushing through the ceiling, out the roof, and floating up into the night sky until they found God. Yet sometimes I saw them bouncing against the ceiling, looking for a way out. As a little boy, that was the best I could do. I don't remember how I solved my puzzlement. I suppose I just went on praying and eventually the concern went away. To this day, however, I sometimes wonder about my words or thoughts or desires or gratitude lifting high enough to reach God. I no longer worry too much about them bouncing off the ceiling, but that vast, seemingly empty and open stretch of stars and darkness can still cause me to pause. I particularly like to approach heaven when I am outside.

God is still, in my mind, situated above me (and I do so want to reach him, as do we all), though I affirm with faith Paul's lovely words from Athens, "In him we live, and move, and have our being" (Acts 17:28). The repetition of those three Vs (*live, move, have*) is magical; it seems to provide an additional witness to Paul's testimony. Paul's conception of where God is seems to be more "around" or "next to" than "up." This is all metaphysical metaphor, but my mind deals best with images and pictures. God must be somewhere; for me he's still above me. I usually look up when I talk to him, though without the barrier of my childhood. I believe our lives are, in a sense, a constant reaching upward toward God.

We must talk with him as did Moses, face to face. This is not only what we long for, but what God also ardently desires. For Moses, that may have meant an actual physical encounter. For most of us, it is an expression that suggests friendship, open communication, honesty, and familiar conversations. Moses' experience was that "the Lord spake unto Moses face to face, as a man speaketh unto his friend"

(Exodus 33:11). God *is* our friend, and friends speak with love, comfort, and trusting truthfulness. It is interesting that later in this same chapter, immediately after Moses asks, "I beseech thee, shew me thy glory," God tells Moses, "Thou canst not see my face: for there shall no man see me, and live" (Exodus 33:18, 20). Evidently "face-to-face" is not always a physical viewing and the phrase should seldom be read literally. I suspect the majority of the time it is more figurative and therefore may be descriptive of us all as we feel after our Father in Heaven.

Abraham "talked with the Lord, face to face, as one man talketh with another" (Abraham 3:11). The phrase is used of Jacob in Genesis as he returns to the land of Canaan (see Genesis 32:30) and of all the children of Israel in Numbers: "They will tell it to the inhabitants of this land: for they have heard that thou Lord art among this people, that thou Lord art seen face to face, and . . . that thou goest before them" (Numbers 14:14). Moses reminded the people that "the Lord talked with you face to face in the mount" (Deuteronomy 5:4). Ezekiel, speaking for the Lord, told of a future gathering of Israel, saying, "I will bring you into the wilderness of the people, and there will I plead with you face to face" (Ezekiel 20:35). *Wilderness of the people* is a compelling phrase that can easily be applied to our own era. The world around us, with its continually deteriorating morals, ideals, values, and expectations, can at times be a true wilderness. Hence the need for us to commune face-to-face and the Lord's promise he will return our desire in kind. It can also mean a place of seclusion—our own wildernesses—just as the children of Israel were led through the wilderness to learn to know the God they worshipped. We are constantly encouraged in the scriptures to seek the face of the Lord. As David wrote, "Seek his face evermore" (Psalm 105:4). This invitation is repeated in the Doctrine and Covenants, "Seek the face of the Lord always, that in patience ye may possess your souls" (D&C 101:38).

God is our Father, is he not? And therefore we may all talk with him face to face. Pascal taught that "God has established prayer . . . to communicate to his creatures the dignity of causality" (Pascal, *Pensées*, 166). He gives us opportunity to join him in his work of creation through reasoning with him. I like that. It tastes good, as Alma or the Prophet Joseph might say. We do address God as our Father; Jesus told Mary in that sacred encounter at the garden tomb that he was ascending to "my Father, and your Father; and to my God, and your God" (John 20:17). The Savior's closeness with the Father is open to us all. I have repeated to myself many hundreds of times Paul's beautiful words from Mars Hill, wherein he says that we are invited to "*feel after him, and find him*, though he *be not far* from every one of us" (Acts 17:27; emphasis added). Again, the rhythmic alliteration somehow gives Paul's words a musical lift that endear them even more to me. This is a book about feeling and finding, about reaching for the Father we trust and love. Paul's "though" seems to suggest the search may not be as difficult as we might make it. Whatever ceilings there may be, they are porous and the fabric thin. Are there not face-to-face possibilities for us all?

WHEN PRAYER IS NOT ENOUGH

If face-to-face possibilities exist for us all, my childhood questions about ceilings and reaching God need to be balanced by a much more real concern. I can best present it with a conversation I had with a woman in our ward. She is a lovely, faithful member who, after experiencing the tragic ending of a friend's life through suicide, approached me and simply asked, "What do you do when prayer is not enough? What do you do when the scriptures don't seem to work and even the temple, with all its comforts, doesn't fill the void?" Here was a mind and heart "feeling after God" and needing face-to-face comfort. I admired her candid—even blunt—honesty and forthright openness. These were questions drawn from deep inside a righteous soul wrestling with the tragic loss of another diligent and committed soul. They forced me to again search my own interior compass. I knew both women and neither one lacked in spiritual intensity or desire to live as God would wish them to live. Her questions troubled what I thought were long-settled experiences in my own life. I thought for many weeks about answers. I ponder and labor with them still. I do not know if others have fought those inner battles of faith, but I suspect many have. Faith is also a gift of the Spirit; if you possess it, thank God for the peace it bestows.

I have volumes of confidence in prayer and the scriptures, from which so many answers to my own puzzlements have come, and the peace of the Lord's House. Yet in spite of all this, I acknowledge the legitimacy of her questions. I maintain that life's solutions are basically simple, as is the gospel (however men tend to complicate it), but our particular experience may throw us into challenges where the oft-repeated formula of prayer, scripture study, church and temple attendance may be just that—an oft-repeated formula—and the proposed solution rendered less powerful by the number of times it is offered for every exigency.

This formula may not address concerns sufficiently for every person. Sometimes simple prayer is not enough: we need a face-to-face finding. We also need to learn how God speaks to us individually, for he comes to us as we are. What do we do? How do we commence? What paths do we climb? How do we feel after God? How do we find him? I hope the thoughts I have wrestled with and found helpful for myself will not seem just another exercise in semantics. I have discovered that our standard approach to the problems and challenges of day-to-day living may be augmented by changing the formula, the words or directions we commonly use. This shifts us into new mind-sets that can guide us into deeper communications with heaven and a better understanding of mortality. At various times in our lives, the ceiling blocking our prayers from heaven may be thicker than at other times. We want to thin it!

REACH HIGH

I have thought much about a phrase Enos used when he so acutely wanted heaven's help. His face-to-face experience is such a wealth of truth. This well-known story really needs no retelling, but a focus on the specific words he used may provide insights we can add to what we understand about Moses' face-to-face experience or Paul's feeling after and finding. After Enos had prayed all day long and into the night, he "did still raise [his] voice high that it reached the heavens" (Enos 1:4).

Reached is an interesting word. It catches our attention. Was this reaching the conclusion of Enos's supplicating, or was it the effort itself? Was it the destination or the road traveled? When seen as the effort, the journey of his soul rather than the ending place, the word *reached* has drawn me like a magnet into deeper reflection. What we are striving for is that at the end of our reaching, heaven is attained and the voice comes into our minds as it did for Enos. This book is about reaching, about the yearning stretch of the soul toward God. I feel a depth of humility even attempting to write about it, but the questions posed by the sister in my ward keep racing in my head.

Reached gives us a wonderful visual image. We reach with our voices, with our desires, with our pouring outs, with our wrestlings, with our asking and seeking and knocking, and with our feeling mind until heaven responds and we meet face to face. It is never easy, but when simple prayer is not enough (and I hope the phrase *simple prayer* will not be misunderstood), we must find the way until we can say, as did Enos, "I did still raise my voice high that it reached the heavens."

A number of years ago, I gave a Time Out for Women presentation entitled "The Fourth Watch." I had no idea the response I would receive from it. It completely took me by surprise. It was a presentation like many others I had given, nothing really special, but for some reason this one struck a resonant chord in many lives. It contained such simple scriptural principles and I thanked the Lord for having shown them to me. It dealt mainly with ways in which the Lord answers prayers and why heaven sometimes seems silent. The focus throughout was on the answers we receive. Since then, I have been asked by many: "What about the other side of the equation? What about the asking, the questioning?" "Are there any 'fourth watch' perspectives in the scriptures on how we communicate with the Lord from our side?" "Am I not getting guidance because I'm going about it all wrong?" In addition, the haunting questions posed by the sister in my ward continue to trouble me; I cannot shake them or settle them in my mind. All of these questions have something to do with feeling after and finding God. God's children do want face-to-face visits.

Though there are many wonderful books and talks on prayer, sometimes the very word *prayer* can get in the way of talking with God because it has so many meanings and images attached to it. So in this book we are not going to explore prayer, nor will I try to encompass my friend's frank desire for understanding with what has so amply been written; rather we will speak about "pouring out," and "wrestling," and being "filled with desire." We will look at "knocking" at the door Jesus promised would open unto us, for those are the scriptural expressions I have found most useful when I have deeply needed heaven to hear, when I have needed to know in my soul that more than my words were being received. That brings us to Hannah's reaching—perhaps the best place to begin.

CHAPTER ONE

REACHING THROUGH POURING OUT

I did pour out my whole soul unto God.

—ENOS 1:9

SUNDAY MORNING BIBLES

I was raised by a mother who taught me that shopping on Sunday was not done except in the most exceptional of cases. I lived by this religiously. Because of this, you can imagine my quandary when the first serious temptation to violate this commandment swept over me one Sunday morning as I looked at the four-hundred-year-old pages lying before me. I have been intensely interested for many years in the history of the English Bible, so when an exhibition of old Bibles came to our community with displays of everything—a handwritten Wycliffe, the Great Bible from an old English parish church, a 1611 original King James edition, Geneva Bibles held dear by the early Puritans, a 1526 William Tyndale facsimile—I was compelled to go see it. They would be in the local high school on a Sunday morning. I couldn't think of a better way to spend a Sunday morning, so I drove down and peered at the precious copies, including a first-edition Gutenberg. So far, so good!

The temptation came as the seminar concluded and the opportunity was offered to buy single pages of torn and damaged Bibles. The prices were far out of my range as a young institute teacher, so I hesitated to even look, but what harm could it do? I might have survived except for two pages that stared up at me from the display case. There was the parable of the prodigal son, my most loved story in all the standard works—in all literature!—taken from a first-edition King James Bible published in 1611. Next to it was the story of Hannah, pleading with the Lord for the son she would eventually call Samuel, recorded in 1 Samuel 1, salvaged from a 1599 Geneva Bible. This was one of my favorite Old Testament stories, one that had blessed my life for years. I love Hannah. I had to have those two pages! Out came the credit card and a faint hope I could justify the purchase to my wife, let alone the Lord. I had them both framed to museum standards and they have hung in our house for many years now. (I made sure I paid off the credit card on a weekday just in case I might get any points with the Lord for that small act of repentance. Laurie and I used to laugh about that justification.) To be honest, I have never really regretted my purchases. I suppose telling this story is a strange way to begin a publication for Deseret Book about feeling after and finding God, but I know no other way of projecting how much the Hannah story means to me. I have taken the chapter title from that story.

HANNAH'S REACH

Hannah had a problem no earthly help could solve. Have you ever felt that way? We are poignantly and briefly brought into her life with the very cryptic introduction, "Hannah had no children" (1 Samuel 1:2). We are quickly told that she had a good husband, Elkanah, who "gave [her] a worthy portion; for he loved Hannah" at the yearly sacrifices held at Shiloh, "but the Lord had shut up her womb" (1 Samuel 1:5). In the world of the Old Testament, everything was attributed to the Lord—in this case, Hannah's inability to bear a child. What the Lord's actual involvement was gives us room to ponder, but Elkanah's other wife, Peninnah, couldn't restrain herself from constantly reminding Hannah of her deficiency. She "provoked her sore, for to make her fret, because the Lord had shut up her womb" (1 Samuel 1:6). There are those fateful words again, so blunt, so suggestive that something was wrong with Hannah. Again, in the cultural thinking of the time, why else would the Lord withhold this righteous and holy desire? This goes on "year by year." I would highlight the words, "provoked . . . sore" and "make her fret" because they are so easy to relate to our own situations from time to time. How many times in my life have things over which I had no apparent control made me fret? How many of us have been "provoked sore," by life or by other people? I have often wondered if God was sending me a trial—crafting my dilemmas—or if life was just happening. I believe that, most commonly, the truth is that life just happens, though we often talk of the Lord testing us or bringing us trials. Generally speaking, mortality brings enough without the Lord's additions. There are, no doubt, some trials that do come from him. Determining which are tailored trials from God and which are not from Him sometimes amplifies our perplexity. Our questions generally increase as time passes; the causes for our fretting seem never to diminish. Because of our experiences, we respond easily to how long this goes on for Hannah—"year by year" sounds so endless.

As the years crawl by, stronger words begin to emerge from the Hannah story, some from Hannah's own mouth. Fretting and being provoked sore are one thing, but what do we do when we feel "bitterness of soul" and have "wept sore"? (1 Samuel 1:10). We are told she prayed at this juncture, but *prayer* is not the term Hannah used. "I am a woman of a sorrowful spirit: I have . . . *poured out* my soul before the Lord. . . . Out of the abundance of my complaint and grief have I spoken" (1 Samuel 1:15–16; emphasis added). Here is a woman perfectly honest with the Lord and with herself. What are the things which are in her soul? Notice the words and how completely we can relate to them. She is filled with sorrow, complaint, grief, and these in abundance. I don't believe that she is bitter in the sense that we attribute to that word, but there might be a bit of accusation contained in her words.

All this she pours out! All this she empties! The soul can be described as a vessel that fills from time to time with various emotions, thoughts, memories, questions, and so forth. The very phrase *pour out* suggests this visual image. I have found it useful to see my soul as a vessel; I often ask myself what it contains before I kneel before the Lord. There is a difference in my approach when I say, "I'm going to pour out my soul to God," rather than "I'm going to say my prayers." There is more intensity, more earnestness, and more honesty. The very phrase suggests there will be no holding back. *Prayer* to me seems to imply only words or ideas. *Pour out* encompasses the world of emotions and feelings. It is helpful to me to understand or recognize exactly what is in my soul. I must be totally honest with myself. Is it confusion, or doubt, or complaint, or sorrow, or love, or gratitude, or guilt, or shame, or worry? I believe what the Father wants from us is the contents of our souls. I sense that unless we pour out, he cannot pour in. We want to make sure we empty everything to make room for what he will give us in return. In deep communication with our Father in Heaven, this pouring out and pouring in binds us to one another. Saint Teresa of Ávila, the renowned, sixteenth-century Spanish Carmelite nun, issued the invitation to pour out with these words, "Avoid being bashful with God, as some people are, in the belief that they are being humble." Do we not have God's own word that we may communicate with him? She continues: "It would not be humility on your part if the King were to do you a favour and you refused to accept it; but you would be showing humility by taking it, and being pleased with it. . . . Speak with Him as with a Father, a Brother, a Lord and a Spouse" (St. Teresa, *The Way of Perfection*, 184).

Sometimes just the relief of pouring out is so great we don't need anything else—the pouring out itself is the answer. I recall many days coming home from work to a frustrated, despondent, even desperate wife at the end of her rope. Five little children can do that to you! I was far too often prone to put on my Mr. Fix-It hat and begin showering her with solutions. So very many times this was not what she desired. I simply needed to listen with a loving and understanding heart. Once she had everything out, my role ended. Often I didn't need to say a word. I just looked at her with empathy. Other days, something wonderful had happened and she just had to pour out her joy. Once again, my own comments were not really essential; it was the outflowing of her soul that was central.

This is not always the case with our Father in Heaven. There are needs that demand answers if they are available. Yet frequently we just need the understanding, patient, and loving ear that listens. So we pour out. At other times, there is a spiritual exhaustion that our Father in Heaven recognizes, and he waits, for a time, for our spirits to prepare for the pouring in. In Hannah's case, "she went her way . . . and her countenance was no more sad" (1 Samuel 1:18). All her fretting, all her bitterness of soul, all her sorrow, all her complaint and grief, all the "abundance," she poured out and left at the Lord's altar. What relief I sense in those words.

We may ask ourselves, "What things in my soul am I allowed, encouraged, or invited by God to pour out?" Whatever we find within ourselves we may pour out, and we should do so with the most open honesty—fears, disappointments, hoped-for fulfillments and dreams, wounds, frustrations, everything. At times I visualize the human heart as something like a racetrack. At the center is the magnetic pull of our deepest needs, desires, anxieties, or questions. But for whatever reason, we spin rapidly around the track in our thoughts and communications with our Father without ever going to those tender center points. The speed of our prayers tries somehow to keep us out of those sensitive places. We do this for a number of reasons. We may not wish to open up old wounds or disappointed hopes and desires. Perhaps we sense our thoughts are inappropriate, or we fear a "no" answer may be forthcoming, or even that there will be no answer. Perhaps we feel we are being selfish or lack faith or will appear ungrateful for all we already have. At times I have said quietly to myself, *But Lord, if I talk of these desires what can even You do?* This may not be a lack of faith, but an acknowledgment that agency may be involved, the limitations of mortality may be involved, or our own faulty perspective may be involved. We might think, *I have gotten myself into this place; what else should I expect?* Perhaps we are afraid the truth will be too painful to hear; it may require a too-threatening openness with self.

Another possibility exists, however. Have you ever thought you were making a mountain out of a molehill? I certainly have. I remember one critical year in our family's life when, after pondering a great deal on a certain dilemma, I finally let my circling talks with God slow enough to be pulled into the center place and I cried out, "Lord, is this such a little concern in thy sight that I shouldn't even bother you with it? Is my own vision the problem?" And after that final, full pouring out, he answered, "If it is important to you, it is important to me." This was not the answer my troubled heart wanted, but I can't tell you how much courage, comfort, and renewal it imparted—and still does.

I will try to illustrate pouring out with a few other examples. I know of no child of God who does not need to, on a fairly consistent basis, simply pour out. We will pray, certainly, and that daily, but in addition to those more casual, not-so-consequential conversations, the heart has need to reveal itself at the pouring-out level. Those informal, intimate talks we have with the Lord throughout the day give us dignity born of the realization that a Being of such majesty permits this familiarity, but pouring out unites us to a Father with the trusting, loving innocence of a child. He becomes our "Abba," as Jesus in Gethsemane cried out to him (see Mark 14:36). As the Lord himself said in Hosea, "I drew them . . . with bands of love" (Hosea 11:4).

REMORSE OF CONSCIENCE

I believe one of the most painful and discouraging things to keep in the vessel of our souls is guilt, or what Alma calls "remorse of conscience" (Alma 42:18). Though Hannah's story does not speak of this often-destructive emotion, I wish to begin with it. This type of regret has its purposes, but of all things necessary to pour out, this is first. Guilt does positive damage when stored in the soul too long. It bars the entry of mercy and peace, which cannot heal when the space is occupied by guilt. God delights in forgiveness. He offers it to us unreservedly and without restraint.

We speak of confession as part of the process of repentance. Confession is, in a sense, pouring out. I am not speaking of ecclesiastical confession, but of the personal moments when we tell God all. Our feelings of failure that create this specific remorse need to be emptied. It is before our Father's throne that we go to empty them. If you are like me, however, even before the Lord I hesitate to speak of those things I have done wrong or failed to do right. I much prefer to say, "Lord, forgive me of my sins," and leave it at that general level. Sometimes I hear the Lord answer, "Why, Mike, what have you done?" Knowing this was coming, I reply, "Well, *you* know." And he lovingly and tenderly responds with, "Yes, but it will do you so much good to tell me." So I pour out my sins. There is such relief in doing this—all the shame, the disappointment in self, the embarrassment, the self-recrimination, the regrets, the fear—even loathing at times—empties with the pouring out. The humility of these experiences is in itself a beginning of the renewing pouring in.

Having been a bishop, I know the relief that others feel when they empty their hearts in confession to a Church leader, but I always felt the majority of this easing was just "getting it over with," as they would often say. The peace was not so much an aspect of the emptying—or even of the repenting—but of overcoming the embarrassment of revealing to another human soul (even a sympathetic one who knows from his own life what sin is) the acts of shame in our lives. I am not convinced that the relief others felt was a sure indication of finally received forgiveness. In many cases God had, in all likelihood, offered forgiveness long before. At times, the very difficult battle of forgiving oneself still continued in spite of assurances that forgiveness had been given. Yet pouring out to the Lord is devoid of this element because we understand he knows all anyway. The relief is purer, more cleansing, not imbued with that tiny sense of pride that hates that another person knows our failings—and hates to know them in ourselves.

Our family loved to explore the canyons and arches of the Moab, Utah, area. We spent a great deal of time hiking and camping there. One day while in Moab we walked into the Moab Rock Shop. (Every time I drive by, I recall this experience and the warm memory always brings a smile to my face.) Inside there were trays and boxes of various minerals, geodes, antiques, blue bottles and mason jars, old farming tools, and more. My youngest son, about eight or nine at the time, was captivated by a particular shiny rock in one of the smaller bins, marked for sale for one dollar. He had to have that rock, but failed to express this to either his mother or me. Instead, he picked it up, put it in his pocket when no one was looking, and walked out with it. That was a small act of dishonesty, but it began to trouble his little heart. As the days went by, that gnawing, gripping pain filled his soul more and more. He thought about it almost hourly. His demeanor changed; he was no longer a happy-go-lucky kid. He hid the rock at home under the paw of a stuffed animal, but it had ceased to give any joy. Instead, it became a reminder of his shame. A rock that cost a dollar isn't, in reality, much to worry about, I suppose, but remorse knows no price value.

His heart needed emptying, but he needed help to do so. He took the rock into the kitchen where his mother was working and began to tap it on the counter. In time, the sound annoyed my wife and she turned and asked him what he had in his hand. He opened his fingers and showed her the glittering stone which weighed a ton in his mind; the tears began to fall. Laurie, guessing the cause, asked our son the question that allowed the pouring out to begin: "Where did you get this, McKay?" Out spilled the story. The two of them sat down to decide what should be done. McKay taught our family one of the purest lessons I know about remorse and cleansing. He decided that he should write a letter to the Moab Rock Shop and return the rock. This was not enough, however; he wanted to include a dollar as payment also. The letter was written, the dollar and rock enclosed, but before sealing the envelope, McKay asked, "What if they don't remember who I was?" He decided he needed to draw a picture of himself and include it as well. We were moved by his picture; he drew a sad face with tears and a downturned mouth. He remembered he had been wearing a Cub Scout hat the day he had taken the rock, and told Laurie he thought they might know who he was if he drew his face with the hat. So the hat was added. With the letter sealed and mailed, our son no longer moped. The pouring in had begun. The full inward tide came a little while later when McKay received a letter from Moab. It read:

Dear McKay,

My name is Cooper. I work at the Moab Rock Shop. [Below this, Cooper had drawn a picture of the rock shop with his own face looking out one of the windows.] Thank you very much for returning the rock you stole. Your Mom and Dad are right—it is very bad to steal. To steal is wrong and it makes you feel badly too.

I am keeping your dollar and sending you the rock. You have paid for the rock now, so now you can feel good. [Cooper had drawn a picture of McKay with a happy face.] Thank you for being so considerate—stop by and see us next time you come to Moab!

Your friend,
Cooper

My son still has that letter, and the shiny rock taped to it. Remorse of conscience—guilt—and moral regrets must not be harvested and stored in the heart. They must be poured out or they tend to grow. With that growth, our perception of their nature can change. Either they diminish through rationalization or, far more frequently, they grow to unnatural dimensions not commensurate with their true seriousness and nature. Our own assessment of our goodness or folly is often woefully inadequate. Remorse is not a stable thing; it moves and shifts and gathers momentum until we open the floodgates and let it pour out into the loving ears and heart of a kind Parent who comprehends, forgives, and pours in peace and solace. This cannot take place when the soul is crowded with self-recrimination. Yet forgiveness is also a growing thing. My family witnesses that growth each time we hold Cooper's letter and the smiles—and their accompanying joy—return. Surely forgiveness is the most beautiful of emotions and the kindest of virtues.

The scriptures are filled with beautiful examples of this type of pouring out. More than this, they contain a longing for the pouring in that follows, and therein is contained their power. The Savior's nature and personality drew sinners to him because they felt safe in pouring out in his presence. Perhaps the most beautiful example is the woman described in Luke 7, who approached him in a public setting with a box of ointment. Though she would also be in the condemning company of Simon the Pharisee, "when she knew that Jesus sat at meat in the Pharisee's house, brought an alabaster box of ointment, and stood at his feet behind him weeping, and began to wash his feet with tears, and did wipe them with the hairs of her head, and kissed his feet, and anointed them with the ointment" (Luke 7:37–38). Her actions brought from the Savior an illustrative parable that assured her of her freedom with the simple phrase, "he *frankly* forgave them both" (Luke 7:42; emphasis added). Yet sensing in her a greater need because she had poured out so openly, trustingly, and poignantly, he reaffirmed his teachings with three further expressions of mercy. She needed a pouring in equal to the pain of her shame, and Jesus offered it to her. Here are the Savior's three declarations, two of them directed to her personally. "I say unto thee, Her sins, which are many, are forgiven; for she loved much. . . . And he said unto her, Thy sins are forgiven. . . . And he said to the woman, Thy faith hath saved thee; go in peace" (Luke 7:47–48, 50).

Isaiah, interceding for his straying people, wrote one of the most touching prayers in the Old Testament, rendered more gentle because of its poetic imagery and intensity: "But we are all as an unclean thing, and all our righteousnesses are as filthy rags; and we all do fade as a leaf; and our iniquities, like the wind, have taken us away. And there is none that calleth upon thy name, that stirreth up himself to take hold of thee. . . . But now, O Lord, thou art our Father; we are the clay, and thou our potter; and we all are the work of thy hand. Be not wroth very sore, O Lord, neither remember iniquity for ever: behold, see, we beseech thee, we are all thy people. . . . Wilt thou refrain thyself for these things, O Lord? wilt thou hold thy peace?" (Isaiah 64:6–9, 12).

Perhaps David gave the most poignant pouring out as contained in the 51st Psalm after his sin with Bathsheba. It has been viewed as the epitome of the penitent heart since it was written so many centuries ago: "Have mercy upon me, O God, according to thy lovingkindness: according unto the multitude of thy tender mercies blot out my transgressions. Wash me thoroughly from mine iniquity, and cleanse me from my sin. For I acknowledge my transgressions: and my sin is ever before me. . . . Purge me with hyssop, and I shall be clean: wash me, and I shall be whiter than snow. Make me to hear joy and gladness. . . . Hide thy face from my sins, and blot out all mine iniquities. Create in me a clean heart, O God; and renew a right spirit within me. Cast me not away from thy presence; and take not thy holy spirit from me. Restore unto me the joy of thy salvation; and uphold me with thy free spirit. . . . O God, thou wilt not despise" (Psalm 51:1–3, 7–12, 17).

Most of us do not have to have the poetic power of an Isaiah or a David, but we are invited to open our hearts as they did and let the love and the longing, the aches and the agonies, reach out for returning compassion. The emptying itself is half the healing. Then we await heaven's rivers of pardon, empathy, and mercy to flow in—which they always will if we let them.

"BITTERNESS OF SOUL— ABUNDANCE OF COMPLAINT"

Hannah's own words spoke of complaint and bitterness. They are strong words. Can one complain before God and not cross over the line of appropriateness? Can one pour out bitterness and complaint, especially in abundance, without offending the giver of so much goodness? Can one protest life's unfairness without inheriting Laman's and Lemuel's soul-sickness of murmuring? We would not criticize God nor find fault with the wisdom of the heavens, yet what do we do when doubt attacks, anger seeps in, or simple confusion bewilders? These, equally with remorse, must not be allowed to remain within.

There are times in our lives when mortality's unkindness and stark realities fill the soul with questions and we may doubt God himself. We may cry out as Joseph did in Liberty Jail, "O God, where art thou?" (D&C 121:1). Yet our faith and need to believe tries to hold on against winds of skepticism, uncertainty, disappointment, and hesitating conviction. Is He there? Is He love? Is He aware? Does He care? The evidence against faith can be at certain moments of our lives frighteningly real. The heart fills with fear, with unease, distrust—and faith feels crowded, even shunned by the bright glare of experience. Hannah's story used the term *bitterness of soul*. The soul may feel during these challenges both the pain-sorrow aspect of bitterness and the anger and accusatory nature it brings. We run exhaustedly around the racetrack of the heart because to slip into the center puts us at odds with God, in the position of counseling him or questioning him on how he runs the universe—or at least our lives.

Years ago while I was directing the LDS institute of religion in Boulder, Colorado, a young woman, about twenty, came through the door needing help. She was diminutive, frightened—like a cornered rabbit—hungry, out of money, and eight months pregnant. She was homeless and had been told by another church, "Go see the Mormons." She was terrified of men, but accepted me because in her mind I was a "reverend." Thus began for me one of those challenging trials of life when we wonder if God really is in his heaven. The story is long and I have detailed it in another publication (see Wilcox, *The Ten-Day Daughter*), so I will only dwell on how it applies to pouring out.

We learned as we cared for her that she had been abused by her father as a child, had run away from home, and had been assaulted by two men next to a burned-out street lamp, her present pregnancy the result of that assault. She had wandered from the Midwest to New England down to Florida and then to Colorado and was absolutely destitute. Over the space of a few weeks we gathered all the Church resources—counseling, doctors, and social services—to help her. She wanted her unborn child to be placed in a caring and loving family, and steps were taken to accomplish this desire. Educational opportunities were offered. But her fear and inability to deeply trust or accept love were always present.

In spite of all our assurances, compassion, and care, one morning she walked out the door, caught a bus, and disappeared from our lives. I had expected what I call an "*Ensign* ending," the sort of stories I read each month in which "charity never faileth." Yet that ending eluded me. I was affected by it more deeply than I cared to admit. All the questions, an abundance of complaint, were in my heart, centering mainly on blaming God for not allowing everything to turn out happy. I couldn't talk to my Father in Heaven about it, but just like guilt, my doubts, uncertainties, and, yes, anger, began to grow. Things that need pouring out of the heart always seem to expand, send their roots deeper, grip more tenaciously, and can often become menacing.

When my ordinary prayers for this lost young woman's protection and welfare could no longer spin around that magnetic center, I heard the Lord ask me a simple question: "Do you think I am not aware of what is in the center of your heart?" Then came the invitation: "Pour it out!" And so I did. *Where were you? Why did you not stop her from running? What will happen to her now? Couldn't you have kept her here long enough for the child to be born and placed in a caring family? What will happen to the baby? Where was heaven's help when we were all trying so hard? Was there no pity looking down on us all?* On and on the questions and recriminations came! In time I was spiritually out of breath, but I got it all out. I sense God's dignity is large enough to take even these kinds of outbursts. I was so full of bitterness, doubt, confusion, and hopelessness there was no room for answers or peace until I poured it out. Then I was taught one of the great lessons of my life as the Spirit simply replaced all that indignation, pain, and disappointment with these words: "What you have done is not lost! Did you need an answer for your love? Was not the giving enough?"

I have talked to a great many people who have doubts about God, Joseph Smith, a literal creation, other religions, the Church's positions on various issues, the Book of Mormon, events in their own lives, and other concerns. I have had serious conversations with wonderful Saints who usually do have some justification for their personal abundance of complaint. We will explore this more intently in another area. Suffice it to say here that inevitably people harbor these thoughts in their souls often without taking them to God, not just in simple prayer, but in pouring out prayer which speaks honestly and lays everything before their Maker. If they become disaffected, despondently discouraged, or overly despairing they often cease to pray at all. Even the very existence of the Being to whom they could pour out might be in question. We have a beautiful example of this manner of pouring out in Alma 22:18, when king Lamoni's father movingly expressed his desire to believe, "O God, Aaron hath told me that there is a God; and if there is a God, and if thou art God, wilt thou make thyself known unto me, and I will give away all my sins to know thee." There is such great honesty in these questing words. Frank sincerity is always a part of pouring out.

Pouring out an abundance of complaint was not unique to Hannah. The scriptures provide many witnesses. I think of Elijah reaching the depths of discouragement after his encounter with the priests of Baal at Mount Carmel. Warned by Jezebel that she would take his life, he fled hundreds of miles to the summit of Mount Sinai. In two verses in 1 Kings 19 we read the exact same words of frustration and complaint from Elijah: "I have been very jealous for the Lord God of hosts: for the children of Israel have forsaken thy covenant, thrown down thine altars, and slain thy prophets with the sword; and I, even I only, am left; and they seek my life, to take it away" (1 Kings 19:10 and 14). It is at this point in his life that Elijah asked God to take his life for he had no hope of success in his prophetic calling. It is at this point, after demonstrations of fire, wind, and earthquake—the outward manifestations of a

God of power—that Elijah hears "a still small voice" pouring into his mind offering comfort and counsel (1 Kings 19:12). The voice's presence assured him God is not "out there," but close enough to be heard as a whisper. The very description of the Spirit as "still [and] small" suggests this intimacy. There is no need for God to shout, or even to call loudly across the room or the expanse of his universe.

Moses was even more open in his pouring out to Jehovah while wandering in the wilderness with the inconstant, wavering, and lacking-in-faith Israelites. When they had complained and rebelled one time too many, Moses had enough. He asked the Lord: "Wherefore hast thou afflicted thy servant? and wherefore have I not found favour in thy sight, that thou layest the burden of all this people upon me? Have I conceived all this people? have I begotten them, that thou shouldest say unto me, Carry them in thy bosom, as a nursing father beareth the sucking child, unto the land which thou swarest unto their fathers? . . . I am not able to bear all this people alone, because it is too heavy for me. And if thou deal thus with me, kill me, I pray thee, out of hand, if I have found favour in thy sight; and let me not see my wretchedness" (Numbers 11:11–12, 14–15). Here is an open, heart-revealing pouring out! And it brings an equal pouring in from God.

"Sorrowful Spirit—Abundance of Grief"

Hannah spoke of sorrow and grief, two words that all humanity will sooner or later come to experience. These are slightly different from the emotional states of bitterness and complaint. The Lord is described as "a man of sorrows, and acquainted with grief." We are specifically reminded that sorrows and griefs were common to man, that the Lord had "borne *our* griefs, and carried *our* sorrows" (Isaiah 53:3–4; emphasis added). I do not read this in a vicarious or atoning sense, but in an experiential one. He truly shared these experiences with us by encountering them in his own life. He understood these things because he chose to be one with humanity, and therein lies his greatest power as a healer. Alma eloquently testified of this truth to the people of Gideon (see Alma 7:11–13).

The story is told in Buddhist lands of a woman named Kisa Gautami whose son had died. She carried his body to the Buddha asking for help. Could he not give her back the child she loved? Moved with compassion, the Buddha told her that, yes, he could give her back her son, but that she needed to bring him four or five mustard seeds from every home in the city in which no one had died. Filled with hope, Kisa Gautami ran into the city, but with each new house she was told this family had also lost one they loved. After a day of searching, she realized that sorrow and grief were common to man and her pain was not unique, though it was *her* pain. She returned to the Buddha, thanked him for his wisdom, and took her son to the river to be cremated.

Eve promised at the very dawn of creation that it was better to pass through sorrow that we may learn from life, for it has so much to teach. I have quoted to myself many times

Robert Frost's brief poem titled "A Question." Therein Frost asks if the pains of life including both physical and those rendered to the soul—life's scars—are too high a price to pay for the great gift of being born. (See *The Poetry of Robert Frost,* 362.)

How would you answer that question? I think we can safely conclude that sorrow and grief seem to be desirable, if not easy to bear, aspects of life's journey—mortal and moral positives, not negatives. We are dealing with a different perspective on life here than we do with remorse of spirit, bitterness, or complaint. We may feel we ought not to complain and wish fervently we had acted in a manner to avoid guilt, but sorrow carries no such negative weight. It is what it is without a moral load attached. This too, however, is to be poured out. We surely must not during these times create unnecessary guilt by thinking, *I should be more grateful. What is the matter with me?*

In truth, we are invited to pour out our sorrows. We find a beautiful example of that inviting in the story of the two disciples on the road to Emmaus. It was Resurrection day and they were confused and troubled by the events of the last few days and hours. "And they talked together of all these things which had happened. And it came to pass, that, while they communed together and reasoned, Jesus himself drew near, and went with them. But their eyes were holden that they should not know him" (Luke 24:14–16). Now here is a comforting truth! Like the two disciples, though our own eyes may be "holden" that we do not understand the Savior's presence by our side, nevertheless he is there, walking with us, communing with us, feeling with us. He asked them a question he asks of us all when we are filled with sorrow: "What manner of communications are these that ye have one to another, as ye walk, and are sad?" (Luke 24:17). This is the beginning of his invitation to pour out. They cannot believe he does not know what has happened in Jerusalem and reply, "Art thou only a stranger in Jerusalem, and hast not known the things which are come to pass there in these days?" (Luke 24:18). Now comes the full invitation for them to empty their sorrows into his empathetic care. He simply says, "What things?" (Luke 24:19). And they pour out! For the next six verses they empty their souls. In similar manner the Savior often comes to us when we are sad, troubled, anxious, or in despair and asks, "Why are you sad, and your communications filled with sorrow?" We might reply, "Are you a stranger, Lord? Don't you know what is happening? I'm facing a divorce!" or "My child is straying from the gospel!" or "I want children and can't have them!" or "I want to be married, but no relationship is promising!" or "I've lost my job and don't know how to take care of my family!"

I must admit there are times when I say, as did the two disciples, "Are you a stranger to my life, Lord? Don't you know what things have happened to me?" Gently he replies, "What things? What is the cause of this sadness in your soul?" Then the pouring out begins and I can say, with unhidden truthfulness, "My beloved Laurie is gone and I am lost in life." He is not a stranger to our grief; there is such a release in telling him all that is in our souls.

I do not believe I really knew what sorrow was until my wife passed away two years ago. Every previous moment of despair paled in comparison. I will not dwell much on this, as I have shared my thoughts in another publication (see Wilcox, *Sunset*). It is sufficient to relate that the sorrow seems to seep back into me after each pouring out. As it builds, I feel the pressure mounting, and my soul aches with all the earliest feelings of loss. Music brings it on, as all songs are now about her, or an old memory will ignite a flood of others, and then I have nowhere to go but to my Father in Heaven and pour it all out. The frequency of this need has often astonished me. I wonder if I have so little hope in the promises of eternity that I should grieve so. Nevertheless, perpetual pouring out is how I survive. So many times when I have poured out my eternal longings, my Father in Heaven has poured in the promises of everlasting reunion. I hope the following two examples will be illustrative.

After Laurie died, each night as I watched the sunset, a familiar despondency would take hold of me. That sinking sun, hung low over the horizon, seemed the final symbol of her life. I wanted to hold the sun in place, but within a few minutes it would slip below the mountain and I would feel the tears gathering. It was always so difficult to watch it disappear, and yet the Lord had earlier given me such consoling words comparing her life to the setting sun and linking it to the promise of a future rising one. Why could I not take them fully into my heart with lasting, not just momentary, peace? One evening when the sorrow gathered around me, I fell to my knees and poured out again all my seemingly never-ending and continually renewing grief. I told the Lord I would not watch any more sunsets. Did I take some kind of perverse pleasure in my own pain? When my soul was empty, as he had done so many times in the preceding weeks, he poured in. With a single sentence sent into my mind, every future sunset changed and became a refreshing symbol of hope: "Each time the sun sets, say to yourself: *I am one day closer to Laurie.*" I do not believe I could have received those words in a soul still so filled with sadness and need that it could not hear the whispered silent voice of the Spirit. But in the hollow chamber of a poured-out heart I could catch its echo. Now each setting sun is a reminder that I am *moving toward* unrestricted, pure-flowing happiness, toward Laurie, not just *moving on* with life. I was farthest away from her the day she died. Each day draws me nearer. Life is full and good and wonderful, worth living every day with joy. Mine is flowing in a direction toward the highest happiness, the most loving fulfillment.

Laurie passed away a few days after Christmas. The last three weeks of her life were spent on a hospice bed in our family room right next to the Christmas tree. In that glad festival of light and color reminiscent of the joy of Jesus' birth, she left mortality. As Christmas drew near again, many of those very painful moments surfaced. Christmas trees are for presents and pine scent, not hospice beds and morphine. I could not set up the tree nor put out the nativity set. The bright lights and merry ornaments took me to places I wished not to go. For me there was a continual pouring out during this festive season. Once again, as with the sunsets, when my soul was empty, heaven's words could come, which changed Christmas for me and restored its celebratory joy. It was a simple thing really. I heard a good friend sing, "I'll Be Home for Christmas" (See *Home for Christmas*). Most of you know the song's lyrics and can imagine how those words touched the tenderest places in my heart. There is a pleading in the song that Christmas remain a time of joy and happiness. I was filled with love as I heard Laurie's voice behind the music. Christmas will now forever be a lesser reunion before the lasting one, a time of overflowing joy and cheer as it was always meant to be. The Christmas tree by which she died became a symbol of anticipation and love with God's pouring in.

"HE SHALL TEACH YOU ALL THINGS"

I have learned the purpose and the power, the need and the hope, of pouring out even when no answer is forthcoming. We stand face to face with God because he always listens and many times that is enough. We feel his compassion or understanding, or his forgiveness, or his acceptance of our love—we receive his divine smile. Sometimes we pour out not because we are going to change God's mind, or because we expect God to make things different, or even because we expect an answer. Our pouring out arises out of our own need. We pray because we must pray, and prayer becomes its own answer. God's listening is the simple restorative for our spiritual health. We depart from heaven's grace as did Hannah—"so the woman went her way . . . and her countenance was no more sad" (1 Samuel 1:18).

In most of what we have explored, the pouring in given by God has consisted of feelings of comfort, peace, forgiveness, acceptance, hope, words of consoling intimacy, but more often than not, I have discovered that the pouring in comes in the form of truth or insight. I recall once studying rather intensely the Savior's teachings to the apostles at the Last Supper. John's account of this is the most expansive, covering almost a third of his entire Gospel. In the midst of so many gracious truths and peace offered by the Lord, we find the Savior's own emphasis on what he calls "the Comforter, which is the Holy Ghost, whom the Father will send in my name" (John 14:26). The title *Comforter* in the past always meant to me the mission of the Holy Spirit to transmit the traditional understanding of this title; that is, the Spirit brings soothing, warming, calming, gently flowing love and mercy to the soul. Having once attached this meaning to the title *Comforter*, I always after thought of these precious gifts in the same frame of mind without looking for additional insight. The Holy Spirit, however, is also a witness of or testifier to truth. I admitted that the two roles overlapped, but still kept them distinctly separate in my mind. But in reading Jesus' teachings during the last hours of his life, I suddenly realized that everything Jesus said about the

Comforter related also to witnessing to the truth, not just causing a troubled soul to "be still." Notice this emphasis in these words of the Savior:

"And I will pray the Father, and he shall give you another Comforter, that he may abide with you forever; *even the Spirit of truth*" (John 14:16–17; emphasis added).

"But the Comforter, which is the Holy Ghost . . . *he shall teach you all things, and bring all things to your remembrance*" (John 14:26; emphasis added).

"If I go not away, the Comforter will not come unto you; but if I depart, I will send him unto you. And when he is come, *he will reprove the world of sin, and of righteousness, and of judgment*" (John 16:7–8; emphasis added).

"I have yet many things to say unto you, but ye cannot bear them now. Howbeit when he, the Spirit of truth, is come, *he will guide you into all truth . . . and he will shew you things to come*" (John 16:12–13; emphasis added).

"He shall glorify me: for he shall receive of mine, and shall shew it unto you" (John 16:14).

Imparting truth seems to be the primary role of the Comforter. The comfort, as we traditionally understand it, must come from the truths taught. These consoling, calming truths may be things we never knew or they may be pulled from memory and applied to the ever-changing condition of our lives. They guide us, or teach us, or show us, or reprove (correct or convince) us as the situation demands. In other Bible translations, *Comforter* is sometimes rendered *Counselor*. I like that! It has face-to-face connotations. This confirms his role as a bringer of truth. Peace and assurance and strength come from his truths.

To illustrate: I mentioned above the passing of my beautiful companion and its accompanying heartache. I cannot think of a more intensive tutorial life has given me than learning to live without her. I have been taught many necessary things. As much as any other lesson, I have learned how to answer a question she once so poignantly posed to me before we were married. When we were engaged and at Brigham Young University, my major in English kept me busy reading literature and writing papers. I also worked two jobs to get us through school. My temperament, whether good or bad, is one where I cannot truly relax until all tasks or assignments are completed. Once they are, I can enjoy doing what I want to do. Anyone can see the trap herein. When are we ever really done? There is always a new project. At any rate, I was failing to spend time with Laurie to the degree she needed. The call of the next novel, or essay, or work shift was always persistent. I recall arriving at her apartment quite late one day when I had not been properly attentive. In the ensuing conversation, I tried to explain that I wanted to be with her much more than I did with Wordsworth, Twain, Tolstoy, or Austen, but the pressure of tests and grades weighed on me tremendously. Close to tears, she simply asked, "But Mike, don't you need me?" I can still hear the pain in her voice, the effort to control her emotions. I was twenty-two, and at the worst really quite stupid and at the best simply foolish. I didn't answer the question correctly. I loved her, I wanted her, but at that point in my life I would not have used the verb *need* to describe my relationship with her. I'm not sure I could even have answered that question correctly when I was sixty. Now she is gone and I know how to reply. Life has taught me. Death has taught me. The Comforter has taught me. Loneliness for Laurie has taught me. I would give up every A I received at BYU to answer that question in her presence, but I did not remember it until after her death. One night, after the urgent pouring out of my heart, I remembered that painful conversation on the front porch of her apartment. I had not thought of it for many years, but it came back with force and brought my own tears. "The Comforter . . . shall . . . bring all things to your remembrance" (John 14:26). Now in my silent conversations with her (which I plead with God he will let her hear), I say, *Laurie, please ask me the question again. I know how to answer it now. I need you like air and sunshine.*

Robert Frost's question has come frequently to mind. I answer his inquiry with a resounding "Yes." All the emotional and physical scars may not be worth the gift of birth alone, but they are certainly worth the learning which follows that birth. Perhaps each pouring out expands the soul a little so the pouring in has more to fill and thus we progress and grow until all meetings with God are face to face.

It is necessary to add that with any of the above pouring outs, one is usually not sufficient. Whether it is sorrow or guilt or anger, the soul may fill again. Life, I have found, contains the constant motion of pouring out. Sometimes the grace we receive from God is the ability to simply continue emptying all that lies within our souls as those things we thought, hoped, or believed we had already cleared, contained, or resolved seep back in.

THE SUPREME POURING OUT

Perhaps the greatest examples of pouring out were those of our Savior in Gethsemane and on Calvary. Isaiah described those moments of more-than-prayer with the brief phrase, "He hath poured out his soul unto death" (Isaiah 53:12). Luke beautifully and simply recorded, "And being in an agony he prayed more earnestly" (Luke 22:44). We know that prayer very well—the pleading that the cup might pass. "Abba," Jesus cried out, which was the intimate, trusting word Hebrew children used when addressing a beloved parent. In the Gospels we witness the Savior's agony in the third person, but in the Psalms we are taken right up onto the cross when Jesus, quoting Psalm 22, asked why he had been forsaken. We then read, "I am poured out like water" (Psalm 22:14). Telling His Father openly all that he is experiencing touches the chords of our heart as we witness, as though we were with him on the very cross, the Savior's pouring out. "All they that see me laugh me to scorn. . . . They gaped upon me with their mouths. . . . All my bones are out of joint: my heart is like wax; it is melted in the midst of my bowels. My strength is dried up like a potsherd; and my tongue cleaveth to my jaws; and thou hast brought me into the dust of death. . . . The assembly of the wicked have inclosed me: they pierced my hands and my feet. . . . They look and stare upon me. They part my garments among themselves, and cast lots upon my vesture. But be not thou far from me, O Lord: O my strength, haste thee to help me" (Psalm 22:7, 13–19).

In the concluding verses of Psalm 22, we hear the Father's answering love: "All the ends of the world shall remember and turn unto the Lord: and all the kindreds of the nations shall worship before thee. . . . All they that go down to the dust shall bow before him. . . . They shall come, and shall declare his righteousness unto a people that shall be born, that he hath done this" (Psalm 22:27, 29, 31).

"IS IT ALL OUT?"

Pour out—that God may pour in! When I served as a bishop and members of the ward would come to me with problems or a need to confess, I would try to listen silently. This was often difficult because it is part of human nature to jump right in and begin solving problems or giving advice. I was far too frequently thinking about how I would respond rather than truly understanding the words I was hearing. This was usually counterproductive because my readiness to speak at times stopped the outflowing of their hearts. I would interrupt that flow. I cannot tell you how often I chastened myself after an interview for not letting someone get it all out before I started speaking. I have found this to be true even with conversations I have with my children, friends, students, or others who just want to talk. It is better to wait for the silence that comes when the soul is really empty after a true pouring out. However, I did learn to ask, "Is there anything else?" Our Father in Heaven is a much better listener than I am. Perhaps the answers or comfort or direction we so earnestly want don't come because the Father knows when there are still things inside that must find an exit. We wonder why he is not answering when he is patiently waiting for us to finish. I think I hear him say to me from time to time, "Mike, is it all out?" This invites me to deeper reflection as I search my soul. It encourages wide-open-door honesty not only with God, but with myself. I think you will agree that often the last bit, so difficult to get out, is usually the one that most needs expressing. That final bit may not, however, always be the most serious, but may bring the highest relief or the most joyful pouring in.

I recall my mother and my Uncle Duna laughing with great delight as they retold what came to be known in our family as the "candy bar story." "Duna" was a Danish nickname given to my mother's younger brother. They were the best of friends when they were growing up, my mother being a few years older than Duna. It was the height of the Depression and treats were few and far between. One day while they were walking, they saw a candy bar on the ground. The coveted treasure was divided, but my mother, wanting more, cut it into unequal portions, one about two-thirds and one about one-third of the candy bar. Duna watched carefully, his mouth watering, and noticed the unequal division, so my mother held the two pieces up, concealing the larger piece with her hand and pushing the smaller one above her curled fingers. "Look," she said, "I'm giving you the bigger piece." The small boy was tricked and both ate their treat. Just like my son McKay's dollar rock, this was not a kingdom-denying sin, but it was always on my mother's conscience as they grew up. During World War II, Duna came home on furlough and Mother, fearing perhaps that the war would take her favorite brother, bought a candy bar and waited for him to come home. As he entered the room, she slapped the penance for her guilt on the table and said, to my uncle's utter confusion and bewilderment, "There's your darn old candy bar!" She then recounted the story, which, of course, he couldn't remember at all. He laughed merrily at my mother's final, perhaps not so humble—but certainly sincere—pouring out. At last, this small irritation to her conscience brought love and peace and perpetual mirth. I enjoyed so much hearing either one of them relate the tale as they would both laugh long and heartily with the telling.

In my own life, I did not handle a situation with my son very well. It was also a trivial matter, but its memory has always stung. After he grew up, married, and was raising his own children, we were talking one day about the seemingly never-ending supply of parental guilt, our fear we are doing it all wrong. It brought back this memory and I told him about it, along with a deep apology for my insensitivity. To my utter shock, he could not recollect it at all! How could he not have stored in his own memory what was so obvious in my own? Had the roles been reversed, the need to pour out would have been just as great if he remembered and I did not. Had he harbored a tiny level of bitterness or anger over my parental fault, this pouring out would have brought the same unity. These scratches on the soul, whether they come from shame, or bitterness, or sorrow, or, as we shall now explore, expressions of gratitude and love, bring such satisfaction when we pour them out and have them replaced by the pouring in.

POURING OUT LOVE

We do not always pour out our spiritual and emotional needs, but also our adorations, gratitudes, and loves. Are these not also needs, in truth? We watch in wonder as Mary anoints Jesus with the spikenard just prior to his atoning hour. "As he sat at meat, there came a woman having an alabaster box of ointment of spikenard very precious; and she brake the box, and poured it on his head" (Mark 14:3). In John's account, she then anointed his feet with the spikenard "and wiped his feet with her hair: and the house was filled with the odour of the ointment" (John 12:3). Though criticized by some of the disciples for her extravagance, Jesus came to her rescue, telling them she had done a good thing, "and this which she has done unto me, shall be had in remembrance in generations to come, wheresoever my gospel shall be preached" (JST, Mark 14:8).

At times the heart is so full of love it spills over, as it did in Bethany that day. This kind of pouring out focuses not so much on gifts given by our Father in Heaven, but on the giver of those gifts, which marks the difference between simple gratitude and adoration. Gratitude centers on the gift, adoration on the giver. I recall being taught the necessity of this type of pouring out one evening during the last months of my mission in France. I had sat down to a dinner of a bowl of yoghurt. I had eaten many such dinners. In fact, I can't think of a day in France when we did not eat some yoghurt. We used to mix in sugar, oatmeal, and fruit, but for some reason this night all we had was the yoghurt without the extras. I gave a very rapid blessing that ran something like this: "Father-in-Heaven-thank-you-for-this-yoghurt-please-bless-it-in-the-name-of-Jesus-Christ-amen." There were no pauses, just a running linkage of words that meant nothing but the habit of saying them. Sometimes we say the closing to our prayers so quickly it becomes one word. I must admit I was not filled with adoration that evening nor even simple gratitude; I was merely going through the motions.

Later that night, through the gift of my imagination, I was taken on a mental journey by the Holy Spirit. During that journey I learned how wonderful it is to pour out love and adoration—even over a bowl of yoghurt. It was a face-to-face encounter I had not felt after, but at its end I did find God. Nephi talked of being carried "upon the wings of his Spirit" (2 Nephi 4:25), and the Doctrine and Covenants tells us that we can "mount up in the imagination of [our] thoughts as upon eagles' wings" (D&C 124:99). Both are beautiful expressions. We fly or soar or are lifted up by the Spirit. I know of no other way to describe this experience.

The first stop was the California coast near where I grew

up. The sun was setting over the Pacific and the sky was radiating color. Orange, coral, pearl, scarlet, and pink shone on the clouds against the backdrop of deepening blue. The sun rode the sea on the horizon for a brief moment, then slipped into the water. I could hear the waves lapping the shore and gulls crying, feel the soft salt spray on my face and the wet sand pulling at my feet as the ocean rose and fell rhythmically. Everything was so serene, so lovely! "With your bowl of yoghurt," a voice whispered, "I give you all the beauty of the earth."

The scene shifted to a more painful memory. I was a fresh young missionary who had been raised in the open opportunity of American middle-class bounty. I was walking in Marseille with my companion when a movement down a back alley caught my attention. There, amid the garbage cans and refuse, was a man. He was pulling himself along the ground on a mechanic's dolly; he had no legs. His fingers seemed fused together with calluses. He was picking through the trash, looking for food. It was my first encounter with gripping, soul-hungry poverty. The voice at my side came again, gently, without rebuke: "With your bowl of yoghurt, I give you dignity, and hope, and security." (I am now sixty-three years old and I have never known a day of hunger. I have fasted, as we all have, but hunger—real hunger—is accompanied by fear and sterile uncertainty. This I have never experienced.)

We moved on to the beaches of Normandy in northern France. There in the American cemetery, the white crosses and Stars of David stretch out in parallel lines across the deep green lawn. The beach below is peaceful now, but once reverberated with the cries of dying men. Through the returning echoes of those voices came the whispered one at my side, which earnestly and again, without reproach, said, "With your bowl of yoghurt, I give you liberty, freedom, and independence—bought at the terrible price of human suffering and sacrifice."

The shores of France dimmed and I found myself back in America, at a stone jail in Carthage, Illinois. It was a June afternoon, the air humid, a sense of melancholy brooding in the atmosphere. I looked up at the window from which the Prophet Joseph Smith fell in 1844. The memory of that day resounded in my soul. I could still faintly hear the strains of "A Poor Wayfaring Man of Grief," then the cries of angry men and footsteps on the stairs. Through the music and the voices, the accompanying presence reminded me, "With your bowl of yoghurt, I give you truth and light which 'cost the best blood of the nineteenth century' (D&C 135:6)."

Then we were at South Pass, Wyoming. The year was 1856. I watched as the Willie and Martin Handcart companies climbed through the snow and wind heading west, always west, toward their dream of Zion. They buried their dead in shallow graves scratched from the frosted soil and continued the long pull to their journey's end. On the fading burden of the wind came the mildly worded pronouncement, "With your bowl of yoghurt, I give you a heritage built on the sacrifices of countless thousands who came before you and bequeathed to their posterity the blessings of chapels, temples, universities—all the fulness of the Church."

The images shifted again and I saw myself as a small boy

sitting on the floor next to my grandfather's green leather rocking chair. I heard the musical murmuring wrinkle of thin paper as my grandfather turned the pages of his scriptures to tell me a tale of prophets, apostles, a Savior—all the heroes and heroines of my childhood and youth. Rising from the whispers of those moving leaves of printed page and the tones of my grandfather's gentle voice, the voice at my side reminded me, "With your bowl of yoghurt, I give you wisdom—six thousand years of shared experience from the lives of humanity's greatest souls."

From ancient voices to the living present we traveled. I sat on the hard wooden benches in the balcony of the Salt Lake Tabernacle, seventeen years old, my knees drawn up, my eyes focused on a man praying at the conclusion of his general conference priesthood session address. President Hugh B. Brown was pleading for me, for me only, it seemed. His words filled the beloved old building, expanding my soul and filling me with courage and a sense of destiny: "O, Father, bless these young men. . . . Let thy Spirit guide them. May it hover over them, shield and protect them. . . . O Father, help these young men who are listening tonight . . . that they will know, that with thy help they need not fear the future" (Brown, 116–17). As his words faded into the chambers of my memory, another voice projected into my conscious hearing, the voice of my accompanying companion: "With your bowl of yoghurt, I give you guidance—a clear path to walk marked by the vision of seers."

By this time humility and praise, the deep appreciation

that saturates and soaks the soul with love, with adoration, began to pour out and I said, "Father, if I may, I should like to bless the bowl of yoghurt again." But there was one more stop on the mind's passage and there we traveled.

To what time and place did we journey? The destination of all voyages, a garden in the Kidron Valley outside of the walled city of Old Jerusalem. I sensed in the darkness the outlines of twisted branches and the heavy trunks of deep-rooted olive trees. I watched the Savior enter Gethsemane, kneel and plead with the Father those wonder-filled words that still have the power to penetrate and trouble the soul with amazement, "Abba, Father, all things are possible unto thee; take away this cup from me: nevertheless not what I will, but what thou wilt" (Mark 14:36). In that reverent stillness, through the silence that speaks higher truths than words, the voice that had filled me to overflowing already now brought the double portion of our birthright with an affirmation and a question: "With your bowl of yoghurt, I give you my Son. What more can I give you to make you happy?"

Then there was a pouring out and a pouring in and I felt like the Nephites who recorded, "No tongue can speak . . . and no one can conceive of the joy" (3 Nephi 17:17). Throughout my life I have been taken on this journey with stops added from time to time as life has progressed, such as a sealing room in the Cardston Alberta Temple as I looked across an altar into the face I most love of all human faces. These spiritual flights of the imagination navigated by God himself bring the most lovely of pouring outs because they never leave one only empty, but filled with a fullness that wants to pour out again and again because it will never be sufficient, will never be enough, worlds without end. Paul spoke of our need to "know the love of Christ, which passeth knowledge, that ye might be filled with all the fulness of God" (Ephesians 3:19).

Jesus was once met by ten lepers who asked him for mercy. This he kindly bestowed by telling them to go and show themselves to the priests as required by the law of Moses. As they went, the desired healing came, but only one of them returned to praise the Lord by falling at his feet in gratitude and adoration. "Were there not ten cleansed?" questioned Jesus, "but where are the nine?" (Luke 17:17). I sense his tone was not condemnatory, but sad and subdued, reflective. This is one of my most beloved stories in the New Testament. I often tell my Father in Heaven, "Among my many failings, I ardently hope that ingratitude or inattention to bestowed goodness will not be among them. Open my eyes where they are closed." We would not be one of the nine. Let us pour out, genuinely, and candidly, even if amongst the ten we are alone in doing so.

I think often of Miss Woodward, my eleventh-grade English teacher, who had such a profound impact on my life. She taught me to love the great literature of the world and the magic that well-expressed, elevated thoughts can have on the mind and soul. At sixteen I could not possibly comprehend the gift she was giving me by teaching me how to draw the lovely and noble truths out of poetry, short stories, novels, the classics. I attribute whatever skill I have developed in reading the scriptures to her training, for I believe they are the greatest literature of all. One year under her tutelage gave me tools for a lifetime. Years after graduation I wanted so much to thank her and returned to San Bernardino High School to find her. Much to my disappointment I failed in my attempt, and to this day I look forward to a future meeting, undoubtedly not in this life, when I will be able to pour out my appreciation and let her know that of the thousands of students she taught over the years, one of them remembers her as the most influential woman in his life outside of mother and wife.

As it is common for us to remember our failures in life, how wonderful it is to hear when in a few instances we were really splendid. These pouring outs to each other are needed, perhaps not for us who do the pouring out as much as those into whose ears the love and appreciation flow. If this is true of our interpersonal relationships, how much more true is it with our Eternal Father in Heaven? If it took me years to comprehend the wonderful bestowal grafted into my mind by an English teacher, how long might it take to fully embrace the truths and gifts instilled in us by our Father in Heaven? I sometimes tell him, "Father, I thank thee for all those things thou hast granted of which I am ignorant and for which I would further praise thee if I had the eyes to see or the heart to understand."

CHAPTER TWO

REACHING THROUGH WRESTLING

Nevertheless Alma labored much in the spirit, wrestling with God in mighty prayer.

—ALMA 8:10

ENOS IN THE FOREST

There is another type of feeling after God spoken of in scripture that clarifies and gives intensity to our face-to-face communications with heaven—wrestling. Now, I do not want to get tied up in semantics, but there is intuitive power in words well used. We sense truth. The narrative of scripture is filled top to bottom with metaphorical language. These metaphors are designed to help us reach deeper levels of mind and soul. If a particular image or poetic expression does not help, we search for others.

For example, the Atonement of our Savior is truly beyond our finite minds to comprehend so it is presented in figurative, representative, or illustrative comparisons—three of the main ones being legal, economic, and healing symbols.

He is our advocate—our lawyer—with the Father. Sin is broken law. There will be a judgment and a punishment or reward. We stand before the bar of God. These are all terms from jurisprudence. We need a defense attorney and Jesus pleads for us. Alma and Paul used these terms, but then Alma was a chief judge and Paul lived in the legal world of the Roman Empire.

Sin is also debt, and we are in danger of the creditors. We are unable to balance the account. Mercy is applied if we forgive our debtors also, as in the parable of the unmerciful servant. Jesus has the means to pay the debt and we go free. We need a redeemer—that word is an economic word though it is so attached to Christ we may not realize it.

Sin is a sickness, a disease which mars the image of God we carry. We need a physician, as Jesus, himself, indicated when he said: "They that are whole have no need of the physician, but they that are sick: I came not to call the righteous, but sinners to repentance" (Mark 2:17). He is the "balm in Gilead" (Jeremiah 8:22). Jesus is the great healer who cures our spiritual leprosy and makes us whole. "If thou wilt, thou canst make me clean," the leper cried. Jesus responded, "I will; be thou clean" (Mark 1:40–41). And so it is with us all!

Personally, I prefer to think of Jesus as a healer. It is less stressful—or painful, I suppose—to see sin as a disease than as a crime or violated law, or as irresponsible or foolish spending. I'd much rather approach the clinic than the court, but any of these three portrayals of Christ's saving grace can be effective. We use what makes sense within our own souls. The same is true of feeling after and finding God, of reaching for face-to-face dialogue. Pouring out, wrestling, knocking at the door, and others are offered as analogy, as comparative visual aids, or linguistic clarifications, or descriptive symbols because things of the Spirit are sometimes beyond ordinary language and understanding. The prophets in the scriptures attempt to put them, like tools, into our hands. They are levers for the soul to lift thoughts to higher awareness and discernment.

We are dealing with the mind-set and soul-preparation that draws us nearer to God, or as Enos said, "I did still raise my voice high that it reached the heavens" (Enos 1:4). That is what we want to do—reach the heavens, learn how to raise our voices high. Pouring out is one way we can raise our voices or feel after God, but *wrestling* is another. As Hannah helped me learn to pour out, Enos has taught me to wrestle. I have often been impressed with the words Enos chose in his small section of scripture, which has become such a favorite to so many. His description of his efforts imparts such intensity—something that is often required of the soul. He is doing more than mere praying (though I hesitate to use the word *mere* in referring to any conversation with God). Though Enos sometimes uses the word *prayer*, his other expressions dominate and give a better understanding of the state of his mind and heart. Sometimes when I need to raise my voice high I ask myself if Enos's words describe what I am doing as I talk with our Father in Heaven. The building accumulation of Enos's narrative is as instructive as any single expression. Here are the words he applies. All emphasis in the verses is mine.

- "I will tell you of the *wrestle* which I had before God" (Enos 1:2).
- "The words . . . *sunk deep* into my heart" (v. 3).

- "My soul *hungered;* and I kneeled down before my Maker" (v. 4).
- "I cried unto him in *mighty* prayer and *supplication* for mine own soul" (v. 4).
- "I began to *feel a desire*" (v. 9).
- "I did *pour out* my *whole* soul unto God" (v. 9)—Hannah's expression.
- "While I was thus *struggling* in the spirit" (v. 10).
- "I prayed unto him with *many long strugglings*" (v. 11).
- "After I had prayed and *labored* with all diligence" (v. 12).
- "I *cried* unto him *continually*" (v. 15).

Intensity, concentration, passion, will, and effort are at work in the three prayer-filled areas that Enos focuses on—his own needs, his desires for the Nephites, and his hopes for the Lamanites. The answers simply *must* come! He won't stop until they do! He wrestles them into being by hungering, struggling, and laboring in the Spirit. I have sometimes asked students if they think prayer is easy or hard. The answers we give to that question are revealing. Sometimes we too must wrestle with the Lord. I think about how different a response we would have to a friend or family member saying, "I must go and pray" than we would if they said, "I must go and wrestle before the Lord."

Reaching through pouring out suggests, "I'm full anvd must get it out." Our hands lift upward, offering to God what we hold. Reaching through wrestling says, "I'm empty and desire filling." The stretching hand searches for something to grasp. That infusion may be a need for wisdom, forgiveness, strength, more intense faith, patience, love, answers, or hope. It may be a need to calm fears, or, as in Enos's case, to draw forth blessings for others as well as oneself. We may wrestle with the best way to help a child or spouse or friend. Whatever the concern, the emphasis will usually rest in the need to be filled, or for God to intervene in our behalf, or to give direction, guidance, and wisdom. We may simply plead with him to solve our problem or to change the mixture of our lives.

We are given a secondary witness of wrestling a little later in the Book of Mormon. "Alma," we are told, "*labored* much in the spirit, *wrestling* with God in *mighty* prayer" (Alma 8:10; emphasis added). There are some of those words again. Alma's efforts were in behalf of the people in Ammonihah and, unfortunately, produced no immediate results. Alma finally left, rejected by the people. But he was instructed to return; upon his second visit he found and converted Amulek and, in time, even his rival Zeezrom. Our wrestlings, like Alma's, may not always bring immediate answers as they seemed to with Enos, though they took him all day and into the night. Yet eventually the desired reply will come. This is especially true when we labor for another we love.

Is It True?—First Wrestle

When I wrestle, to use Paul's words, I'm "feeling after" something to hold tightly to, to lock firmly into my heart. I was raised by a mother who had a powerful testimony of the Book of Mormon. I can't remember going into her bedroom to say good night and not seeing the Book of Mormon on her nightstand. I recall her reading it intensely, which she does to this day at ninety-one. She read its stories to my sisters and me as young children. It had been the key to her own conversion as she struggled out of inactivity and rebellion. Because of this, I never doubted its truthfulness and I fully anticipated that the outcome would be positive when at the age of fourteen I decided to read it independently and gain my own witness.

However, for whatever inexplicable reason, as I started to read it I was filled with darkness. Doubts seemed to consume me. I was troubled by just about everything—the long chapters quoted from Isaiah, the emphasis on war strategy, phrases from the New Testament, horses, words that appeared to me to be made up like *ziff, cureloms,* and *cumoms.* So I wrestled. I wanted to believe. I wanted it to be true. I could not understand why I wasn't feeling the warm, swelling, burning promises. All was confusion. All was doubt. I sometimes physically trembled with a gripping fear that at certain moments was terrifying. How could my mother be wrong? How could the wonderful people and organization I loved have arisen out of fraud and deception? When I read the Joseph Smith story, I could not help but think *This boy is telling the truth.* But a testimony of the Book of Mormon wouldn't come. It was the black hole in my spiritual universe that was drawing all the light out of me. But I couldn't give up the search. I couldn't just walk away. That book wouldn't leave me alone. The name *Anti-Nephi-Lehies* caused a crisis for me one summer. I was working at my uncle's ranch. We always took Sunday off and I was reading the Book of Mormon in the front room alone—trying once more to get my answer. I never felt that God was saying to me, "It is not true." I just could not shake the night around me when I read it. Sunrise would not come. Maybe it would today. As I read the name *Anti-Nephi-Lehies*, my heart froze. The voices inside me kept saying, *Joseph Smith made that up.* I shut the book and went down into the willows by the river and wrestled with my doubts all day. I pleaded with God, but after hours of pleading, I had to admit to myself that nothing had come. I thought, *Well, maybe in seminary my faith will rise.*

I studied the Book of Mormon in seminary during my senior year. It was not a good experience. I suppose it was partly my own fault, perhaps I was a bit rebellious, but the teacher could not connect with me or hold my attention. It was an early-morning class, and I finally asked my mother if I could drop it. She always gave us children a wide latitude of freedom, and though she was saddened by my choice, she gave me permission. However, the bishop was not so acquiescing. He came to our house and pointed out I was older and needed to set a proper example. I returned, but felt nothing. I did, however, begin to study Maya archeology, thinking maybe there would be something there.

After graduation, I went to Brigham Young University and took a Book of Mormon class. I thought I had the worst teacher in seminary, but my experience at BYU eclipsed even that. I was seventeen and, though it may sound strange considering my lack of Book of Mormon conviction, I never considered not going on a mission. I had planned on one since I was a small boy. I left off studying the Book of Mormon and switched to the Old and New Testaments. As my nineteenth birthday approached and I submitted my papers, I began to talk with returned missionaries, asking them how to be successful. I took a little spiral notebook and wrote down all their suggestions. I had many wonderful ideas, but something seemed lacking. In spite of my failing wrestle with the Book of Mormon, I had faith in a loving God.

One night I knelt beside my bed with the spiral notebook and laid it out before my Father in Heaven. *I have collected all these ideas*, I told him, *but I feel something is missing. If you were to add anything to my list what would it be?* It was such a simple request, but for reasons that were never fully revealed to me, the God we worship chose this moment to end my years of wrestling. With a voice as audible as the Spirit can offer without literally penetrating the ears, I heard these words: "Bear testimony that Joseph Smith was a prophet of God—and that *the Book of Mormon is true.*" Why did I not receive those words when I was fourteen, or in seminary, or at BYU? Why then? Why at a time when I was not even asking for faith to end my long fight with the darkness of doubt? I cannot answer that. God has his ways. Maybe I needed to show the Lord how much I wanted his affirming voice. I do not know, but I went to France and could sit before those we taught and tell them while looking fully in their eyes that I knew Joseph Smith was a prophet and the Book of Mormon was true. Sometimes they would ask me how I knew this and I would answer, "Because the voice of God declared it unto me."

Yet my wrestle was not over, even though I believed it was. How could I have a stronger testimony? What could possibly shake it out of me? As I read the Book of Mormon during my mission, I came to love its stories and truths at a deeper level than when I heard them as a child from my mother. It was the first thing I wanted to get into the hands of those we met. I remember being impressed to put a copy of the Book of Mormon in the mailbox of a woman who told us her husband was not interested. She was converted by reading it alone without missionaries to teach her. My confidence in this wonderful book increased, yet there would be a final struggle.

As my mission neared its end, we were teaching a number of wonderful investigators. They all seemed to be progressing well. But over a period of about a week we lost all of them, and each time the reason was identical: They could not accept the Book of Mormon. We had one final family we were teaching, a single mother, about my own mother's age, raising her children alone. She was such a beautiful person in spirit. I wanted to see her conversion as deeply as any I had taught in France. We approached her door one day and saw a letter taped to it. She told us she loved our church and its people, but she could not see us again. She had decided she could not join because of the Book of Mormon. Many of her concerns resounded in my soul; I knew them well. As we rode our bikes home in the darkness, through my tears I could feel the old fears resurface. I could not contain the thought that if we did not have the Book of Mormon, this woman would be a member of the Church. I found myself wishing it did not exist. You cannot be a good missionary and think that. You cannot be a good member and think it. When my companion was asleep, I knelt and wrestled. I was losing something extremely valuable to me and I did not know how to retrieve it. Finally, exhausted emotionally, I tried to sleep. In the early hours I was granted a dream.

An Old Woman at the Gate

I was in a foreign country with three friends. We were in a small medieval European village, such as you might find a few centuries ago. We loved the people and they loved us. It was a tangible, abiding, enduring, heart-filling love. During the day we labored side by side with them. At night a curious thing happened. They would lock us in a cage for fear we would leave them. We did not mind this nightly ritual because we knew why they were doing it. I have often pondered on this image and thought how powerful it is. If the nations of the world truly understood who the missionaries were that labored among them and what the truths they carry could do for them, would they not do all they could to keep them?

One evening as the door was being locked and we were alone, one of my companions said: "Tomorrow we must go home." He then laid out the escape plan, and as I listened I knew it would work. We were all sad, but I knew also that he was right. We had to go home. It was time. The scene then changed. It was the next morning and the four of us were running down the main street of the town. We had small backpacks on and a crowd of villagers was running after us. Others were leaning from their windows, watching our running figures in desperation. All were crying, as was I. "Why are you leaving? We love you! We have been kind and good to you! We need you! Please don't go!" We were running to the city's entrance gate, a medieval-looking doorway with towers on both sides. The gate was open and once we were through, the people could not follow. I watched my three friends run through the opening, but when my turn came I could not go.

I saw an old woman sitting by the side tower. She had been an especially kind and dear friend. She was weeping; I could not run past that beloved face without stopping. I had only a few seconds before the crowd would overtake me. I knelt on the cobblestones in front of her and removed my backpack. I reached in, removed a French copy of the Book of Mormon, and placed it in her hands. "I can't tell you why I have to go," I said, "yet you must believe that I need to depart. But I want to give you something. It is the most precious thing I have and I love it with all my heart. If you will read it and teach it to your people, it will bring you more happiness than you believe can exist in this world and you won't need us anymore." I rose from her side and ran out the door.

I woke up at this point, all the images bright in my memory. And even more important, the feeling, the love, the conviction, the deep-seated belief was still there. It has never left me since that night. I cannot hold a French copy of the Book of Mormon without being overcome with emotion. I have now taught the Book of Mormon almost every year for the last thirty-five years. I have taught many bright, intelligent, and talented college students over those years, and I can say I have yet to meet the twenty-three- or twenty-four-year-old who could produce it. Its truths have lifted my life. It is one of the central pillars that hold up the ceiling of my soul. I believe that my many wrestling, laboring, long-struggling, hungering cries over the years have anchored it into place.

PILLARS OF THE SOUL

I have related these experiences at length because they represent my greatest wrestle with God, one of my most intense "feel after him" challenges. I have fought my way through two more almost equal in intensity. I have shared them in other publications so I will only briefly refer to them. My first experience with the temple endowment filled me with the same fearful nighttime tossing and darkness. I wished at the time we had no temple ceremony. I had to learn how to understand the symbols that the Lord uses in his house to teach us. This took a number of years and a good deal of thought. When I had wrestled my way through doubts and bewilderment, the temple became beautiful and filled with love and wonder. The highest summit of my life took place in the temple when I was sealed to Laurie.

I anticipate no greater blessing will be bestowed on me in mortality.

I think often of the interior of the soul as a beautiful building held up by masterfully carved pillars that represent those irreplaceable truths we all fervently wish to know with unshakable firmness. There is a loving Father who watches us and cares; his divine Son showed us through his life and teachings and mercy how to live and find a place in our eternal home; that Father and Son spoke to the boy Joseph Smith in a grove of trees and initiated the restoration and revealing of divine truth whose crowning splendor is the temple; the scriptures contain the light and guidance sufficient to bring us home; we are still blessed with prophets and apostles, seers whose vision will be a constant stabilizing comfort as we walk the path that lies before us.

My love for Jesus and his teachings—no lovelier, more beautiful man ever walked the earth—is as solid as I believe it can be in this life, and my faith in my Father in Heaven was born in my earliest childhood and has never been questioned. These pillars have always stood firm, but I would say that two of the strongest supports of my testimony are the Book of Mormon and the temple ordinances. Perhaps in his divine wisdom, God knew that only by wrestling could I shape and raise those pillars into place.

Now I wrestle once again with the passing of my wife. All my happiness depends on the strength of my earlier raised and positioned pillars. If all I believe in is not true, I will never see her again. That is a black hole as great as I have ever faced. I believe my earlier wrestlings have prepared me for this last—and perhaps greatest—struggle my faith has had to sustain. As the Lord brought me through my earlier wrestlings, I trust he will bring me through this final hungering. I wrestle to continue moving along the path of conviction and faith I learned from Dante: "Thus I believe, thus I affirm, thus I am certain it is" (see Browning, "La Saisiaz," 61). We all want to advance from belief to affirmation to certainty, and we will as we feel after, reach for, and in time meet God face to face. We all will wrestle. If you never do, you may thank God with fullest praise that you were given the priceless gift of faith, for it is a gift of the Spirit. For those who wrestle—from the deepest doubts to how to best raise a child or build an eternal marriage; from rising through hope and forgiveness to the approach of an uncertain, perhaps even fearful, future—the Spirit seems to testify, "Don't give up. At the end of your labors the answers come and the pillars erected are stronger for having wrestled them into position." Did not the Lord tell Joseph Smith when he was struggling in Liberty Jail, "Hold on thy way"? (D&C 122:9). May our feet stay on the path—all good things in life lie on the path—and never leave it, though it requires us from time to time to wrestle, to hunger, to labor in order to move forward.

WRESTLING'S SOMETIME IRONY

Perhaps the most well-known use of the verb *to wrestle* in connection with prayer is in the Old Testament, in the story of

Jacob's relationship with his brother Esau. The story is instructive because of the irony of Jacob's awareness—or lack of it. Jacob, returning with his wives and children from two decades of laboring for Laban, hears that his brother Esau is coming to meet him. Believing that Esau is still estranged from him because of their father Isaac's blessing, he throws himself on the Lord's mercy. "Deliver me, I pray thee, from the hand of my brother, from the hand of Esau: for I fear him, lest he will come and smite me, and the mother with the children" (Genesis 32:11).

Later that evening, after having sent his wives over the Jabbok ford, "Jacob was left alone; and there wrestled a man with him until the breaking of the day" (Genesis 32:24). Though the story in Genesis is layered over with other details which can confuse the experience, Hosea's retelling of Jacob's famous wrestle gives clarification. He simply records, "He had power over the angel, and prevailed: he wept, and made supplication unto him" (Hosea 12:4). This is a spiritual wrestling. Jacob prevails as it lasts through the night. It is here that his name is changed to *Israel*, which means "to persevere with God."

Wrestling, in a scriptural context, is by its very nature an upward path whose summit ends with face-to-face meetings, and it can and usually does take perseverance. It is also in this story that we find the first use of the phrase *face to face* in the Bible as it refers to an intimate contact with Deity. As the morning broke, Jacob named the place *Peniel*, which means "the face of God," concluding, "I have seen God face to face, and my life is preserved" (Genesis 32:30).

However powerful the story may be as an illustration of wrestling for God's intervening mercy, there is an even greater truth found in the irony of the story. That irony is one I think about every time I am driven by my needs into the world of feeling after and reaching as did Enos and Jacob. Jacob never needed to anguish so deeply and plead so earnestly for God's protection against Esau. Esau is not estranged! He is not coming to slay Jacob's family. In Jacob's fear, he projected the worse outcome of his impending meeting with his brother—but Esau had only forgiveness, love, and welcome to give. Though Jacob did not know this, the Lord did.

What follows is, next to the forgiveness of the prodigal son, the most soul-lifting and beautiful example of reconciliation and mercy in the standard works. It is on par with another beautiful story of forgiveness in Genesis, that of Joseph and his brothers. "Jacob lifted up his eyes, and looked, and, behold, Esau came, and with him four hundred men. . . . And Esau ran to meet him, and embraced him, and fell on his neck, and kissed him: and they wept" (Genesis 33:1, 4). I have wondered at times when I wrestle, struggle, labor, or hunger for God's help, if there is really no need to if I could only see right. So I have learned to question my questions, fear my fears, and doubt my doubts. That is good for the health of one's spirit.

We will all wrestle throughout our lives. It seems to be a common portion of the cup of mortality. Peter, who walked on the water and then fell with the wind and waves, has comforted me often enough. That story is a perfect portrait of the wrestle between belief and faith and doubt and fear. Sometimes we can walk and sometimes we fall through that thin filament of faith's firmness lying on the surface of the water. Thomas needed to see and feel and even the other apostles, with the Savior standing right in front of them, "yet believed not for joy, and wondered" (Luke 24:41). They needed the added assurance of watching the Master eat a broiled fish and honeycomb. We could talk of Zacharias's hesitant questioning of Gabriel in the temple when John the Baptist's pending birth was announced, a hesitation which brought on his loss of speech and hearing until Elizabeth delivered the promised child. And I think all of us understand a father's plaintive cry to Jesus in behalf of his diseased son, "And straightway the father of the child cried out, and said with tears, Lord, I believe; help thou mine unbelief" (Mark 9:24).

We must be careful that we do not take counsel from our fears, though we are allowed the comfort of knowing that fear is a common part of humanity's struggles. We may believe we are wrestling with the Lord when we are wrestling with our own anxieties. When I am confronted by this possibility, I am always reminded of a scriptural principle I call "ten-piece promises." Herein we will discover another type of reaching.

CHAPTER THREE

REACHING THROUGH BELIEVING

For we are made partakers of Christ,
if we hold the beginning of our
confidence stedfast unto the end.

—HEBREWS 3:14

TEN-PIECE PROMISES

Sometimes we wrestle and reach to obtain—and sometimes we reach and wrestle to keep or hold fast to what we have already received and may lose without constant vigilance. Having found God and received his promises, we do not want to then lose them. During the last years of Solomon's reign, he discovered a remarkable young man named Jeroboam, whom he made "ruler over all the charge of the house of Joseph" (1 Kings 11:28). One day while leaving Jerusalem, Jeroboam was alone in a field, and a prophet named Ahijah caught up to him with a message from the Lord. In Old Testament times, prophets would do symbolic, visual, theatrical acts that caught everyone's attention. Many were quite dramatic and not easily forgotten, which was just the point.

Jeroboam had on a new garment, "and Ahijah caught the new garment that was on him, and rent it in twelve pieces: and he said to Jeroboam, Take thee ten pieces: for thus saith the Lord, the God of Israel, Behold I will rend the kingdom out of the hand of Solomon, and will give ten tribes to thee"

(1 Kings 11:30–31). This story is the beginning of what we have called the ten tribes of Israel ever since. It was not, however, the end of the message. There were promises that went along with Jeroboam's new leadership: "Thou shalt reign according to all that thy soul desireth. . . . And it shall be, if thou wilt hearken unto all that I command thee, and wilt walk in my ways, and do that is right in my sight, to keep my statutes and my commandments . . . that I will be with thee, and build thee a sure house, as I built for David, and will give Israel unto thee" (1 Kings 11:37–38).

The Lord's words were as plain and straightforward as they could be. Jeroboam would establish a ruling dynasty over Israel that would be long-lasting, and he would have all his soul's desires. With this, Ahijah left Jeroboam to ponder in the field. I can see him standing alone, contemplating the ten pieces of cloth and the future they represented. Of course, as with any covenant with God, there was an all-important "if." Perhaps Jeroboam wondered at this point how it could all come true. Solomon was king and the kingdom would pass to his son. But in a rapid progression of events, Jeroboam fled to Egypt (to escape the now not-so-friendly Solomon, who sought his life), Solomon died, his son Rehoboam took over, and there was rebellion in the wind. Returning from Egypt, Jeroboam led a delegation from the northern tribes to ask Rehoboam to ease the taxes Solomon had put upon them. Instead of listening to the wisdom of the elders in his court who counseled moderation, Rehoboam followed the foolish young men he grew up with and decided to get tough with

the rebellious northern tribes. He would be more tyranni-
cal and exacting than his father. "What portion have we in
David?" they asked; "to your tents, O Israel" (1 Kings 12:16).
The Hebrew nation split and the ten tribes, as Ahijah had
promised, chose Jeroboam to lead them. All had come about
as foretold.

Yet Jeroboam made a mistake as costly as Rehoboam's—
he took counsel from the wrong source. In his case, the
source was the worst of all possible counselors—his fears!
One should make decisions based on faith, not fear. This is its
own type of reaching. Choices made in fear are usually poor,
and their consequences can be widespread and often cata-
strophic. Jeroboam began to wonder what his chances were of
really establishing an independent nation and ruling dynasty.
Rehoboam had the temple; he had Jerusalem. He had the
right of succession handed down from David to his father,
Solomon, on his side as well.

What did Jeroboam have that could possibly outweigh
those heavy draws? The scriptures respond: he had the Lord's
promises! He had ten pieces of cloth! Here was a need to feel
after and find God, to reach and wrestle, and, if nothing else,
to pour out his fears. "And Jeroboam said in his heart, Now
shall the kingdom return to the house of David: if this people
go up to do sacrifice in the house of the Lord at Jerusalem,
then shall the heart of this people turn again unto their lord,
even unto Rehoboam king of Judah, and they shall kill me"
(1 Kings 12:26–27).

This was the time for Jeroboam to retrieve his ten pieces

of cloth, draw them across his hand and pull strength from them, remembering those moments in the field with Ahijah. There have been many moments in my life when I have had to, figuratively, pull out my ten pieces and hold them lovingly in remembrance. We need to recover our newly born faith, created when we were given promises and our crisis of faith was still in the future. What God promises, God fulfills. That is one of the certainties of the universe. That is what a ten-piece promise is. There is comfort in holding tightly to those bits of cloth, to remember.

Yet this often requires as great a wrestle, as high a reach, as obtaining those promises or guidance in the first place. Sometimes this is where our wrestling is the greatest. It does not always come in the beginning. Jeroboam's house would rule Israel—Ahijah had said so. He could have all the desires of his heart—Ahijah had said so. But responding to his fears instead, he built two new shrines in Bethel and Dan to rival Jerusalem's temple and set up twin golden calves for the people to worship. These would be his kingdom's gods; the tribes would not desert him for his Davidic rival. They would not need the temple. That was Jeroboam's theory, at any rate.

I love irony in either literature or scripture, and God often uses it to teach his profoundest truths. This story contains the sad but compelling, memorable irony of watching Jeroboam create the very problem he feared. When the Levites would not go along with his new gods, the king replaced them with men who would sacrifice to the calves. The Levites promptly left for the kingdom of Judah and

Rehoboam's rule. "And after them out of all the tribes of Israel such as set their hearts to seek the Lord God of Israel came to Jerusalem. . . . So they strengthened the kingdom of Judah and made Rehoboam . . . strong" (2 Chronicles 11:16–17). Jeroboam's own fear-inspired actions launched the migrations. At a later time, when Judah was ruled by Asa, we read that the draining of the righteous from the northern kingdom was still ongoing, "The strangers with them out of Ephraim and Manasseh, and out of Simeon . . . fell to him out of Israel in abundance, when they saw that the Lord his God was with him" (2Chronicles 15:9).

Jeroboam's house ruled Israel for only two generations and was then replaced through a coup. The northern kingdom never recovered from his fear-inspired choice. The golden calves stayed and the flight of the righteous continued. At one point, a fortress was built to stop the exodus into Judah in an Old Testament forerunner of the Berlin Wall. The north never had a righteous king, and with each new coup, each new reigning house, the scriptures tell us over and over again that the monarch "walked in all the way of Jeroboam . . . and in his sin wherewith he made Israel to sin" (1 Kings 16:26). Generations later, when the ten tribes were led away captive by the Assyrians, Jeroboam's decision was given as the main cause that led to the captivity and eventual scattering wherein the northern kingdom became the lost ten tribes. "For the children of Israel walked in all the sins of Jeroboam which he did; they departed not from them; until the Lord removed Israel out of his sight" (2 Kings 17:22–23).

We speak often of the lost ten tribes. If we asked who lost them, which I think is a more helpful question than where they are, the answer would have to include the fear-inspired decision of a man who was promised everything, but whose reach failed and whose wrestle was lacking. There was no face-to-face feeling after or finding. Rather than pouring out his fears, he harbored them until he created the very problems he most dreaded, then passed them on to succeeding generations with traumatic results. Sometimes when we fail to reach for ourselves, we fail for the thousands who will follow in the culture we create.

Ten-piece promises may come to us in patriarchal blessings, or in words spoken at general conference, or in the scriptures, or to our open, receptive minds when in righteousness we stand in the field to receive them. But ten-piece promises, though compelling, desired, and given in the most faith-promoting of environments and from the most trusted of sources, still often require wrestling and reaching to hold them tightly in our hands. This is especially true when outside forces seem to argue against their fulfillment. Sometimes the wrestling is between the heart and the head, between the Spirit and more worldly reasoning. I have sat many times on the stairs leading up to the platform built for Jeroboam's golden calf at Dan in northern Israel, and the place never fails to fill me with both sadness and resolve. It represents a hinge which turned the destiny of the tribes of Israel. Each time I visit those steps, I leave determined to wrestle and reach, to believe and hold tight to my ten pieces, for our wrestlings may have consequences far wider than we can possibly conceive. Generations may depend on them, and therefore all our labors will be worth our highest reaching. Our face-to-face feeling and finding may bless the lives of our children and theirs. Believing in ten-piece promises may be our highest reach of all.

"Walk without Fear"

I was taught the truth of ten-piece promises when I was a teenager, before I had ever heard the story of Ahijah and Jeroboam's meeting in a field in Israel. I was one of the youngest and smallest boys in my class as I advanced through elementary school, junior high school, and finally the last three grades of high school. Sport was certainly not my element, nor was being comfortable in social settings. I had cracked my upper jaw when five years old playing on a cannon outside the town hall one Sunday morning when I should have been sitting next to my mother in stake conference. I had pestered her so gravely that she relented and let me go and climb the cannon. I ran back into the meeting covered in blood. The result of this, other than being a tremendous embarrassment for my mother, was the formation of a cyst that ate a large hole in the bone just above my front teeth over the next years. We discovered this when I was beginning the eighth grade. A few operations later and I was outfitted with braces and a gaping hole in my smile. I endured that toothless smile for about four years until finally, in the eleventh grade, I was fitted with a permanent bridge. My experience did not make me eager to conquer the world of dating, parties, pretty young women, or any sport where a blow or a fall could cause greater problems with an already woefully deficient smile. I was also the recipient of frequent bullying, which kept me in a pretty constant state of fear. I hated school! After kindergarten, it was all downhill until college. I went to school afraid almost every day. I halfway survived by reminding myself that I could at least ride a horse better than anyone in my Southern California classes because I had spent every summer for as long as I could remember on my uncle's ranch in Nevada.

In light of my deficiencies and experiences, it was a remarkable thing to me that in my patriarchal blessing, which I received at the age of twelve, I was given the following counsel and accompanying assurances: "Keep thyself clean and pure from the sins of this generation, and thou shalt walk without fear." Living in Southern California in the sixties did present a few sins to a young man. I had a fairly good idea what he was talking about. He said a few more comforting things and then some remarkable—to me—promises. I would have the opportunity to be "a light and influence" to those who crossed my path and with whom I associated. The thought of anyone paying much notice to me other than the sort of negative attention I was used to was a bit of a mystery, but there it was for me to read whenever I perused my blessing. Then the patriarch spoke other amazing words: "In thy purity thou shalt seek and find thy helpmate, likewise pure, clean, and undefiled." This was a marvelous thing to me because as the words were spoken I pictured in my mind a very beautiful girl and yet I knew, absolutely knew, I would not marry anyone really beautiful because, after all, what was I to look at? How could I presume to think I could attract such a lovely and talented creature as my imagination created? I had basically already accepted the reality of not marrying the girl of my dreams. Yet there was that promise with its accompanying image.

As I matured, I tried as best I could to follow counsel and believe in the promises and control the many fears that were circling my heart. I would read my blessing, clutching it as Jeroboam might have clutched his ten pieces of cloth. One day in Miss Woodward's English class, of whom I have already spoken, we were discussing Dante's *Divine Comedy*, wherein he takes a journey through hell and heaven. I was a junior in high school. Miss Woodward said that Christianity believed in a heaven and a hell and you either went to one or the other. I don't know what induced me to raise my hand and simply say, "Not all Christian churches believe in just two places one goes to after death." Miss Woodward was always interested in having her students express and defend their views. She knew my older sister and I were Mormons. She turned to me and said, "Oh, Mister Wilcox, and what do you believe?" I don't think in today's educational environment she could get away with such a question, but there I was with the teacher I most idolized in the world asking me what I believed. I tried to explain the three degrees of glory briefly.

She then turned to the class and asked, "Is there anyone here who would like to ask Mr. Wilcox anything about what he has just described?" There were Jewish students, Catholics, a Chinese Buddhist, and many different Protestant denominations represented; for the last forty-five minutes of class I was pounded with questions and challenges. During the entire period, Miss Woodward sat calmly on her stool, watching without saying a word. Just before the bell rang to end my ordeal, she stopped the discussion, looked at me with a slight smile, then turned to the class and said, "We have had a great deal of fun at Mr. Wilcox's expense; but today we have witnessed a rare example of courage. How many of you would have defended your faith as competently and clearly as he has done this morning? Well done, Mr. Wilcox!" Coming from the woman I most admired in all the world short of my mother, these words astonished me. I would never have described myself as a boy of courage, but I realized that morning that I truly could walk without fear and God had kept his promise.

I have over the years done a great deal of public speaking in many different venues—firesides, sacrament meetings, Education Week, BYU Women's Conference, and Deseret Book's Time Out for Women conferences. I spent my life as a teacher, mainly at the institute level, instructing tens of thousands of classes over nearly four decades. I do not refer to this by way of boasting (I have been immeasurably blessed by the opportunities), but to illustrate God's commitment to ten-piece promises. Before I speak, I will often seek a quiet place to be alone and calm my heart, which always beats faster prior to a public address. I can feel my body temperature rise and my mind go completely blank. When I was a small boy I dreaded—hated, really—the day I would be asked to give what were then called two-and-a-half-minute talks. I was simply terrified of speaking before people. I recall many moments when I sought the refuge of the classroom corner when I knew the teacher would assign one of us children to speak. *Please, let it not be me!* was a frequent prayer. I was once told that next to dying, fear of public speaking is the most common phobia people endure, and I believe it. I am often asked before I speak, "Are you ever nervous?" My answer is, "Always! There's never been a time I was not nervous." Yet when I stand and hear my own voice beginning, calm settles into me, the fear fades, confidence and comfort replace the tangle of nerves and dullness of mind, and I enjoy the moment. I truly do! God keeps his promises. I have thousands of witnesses over many years in a multitude of different settings of that truth. He told me I would walk without fear, and though I have said a hundred times, "I don't need to ever speak again"; yet when the invitations come, if I am free, I always say yes. Perhaps if I said no because I doubted the promise, like Jeroboam I would create the very thing I fear and speaking would become the nightmare it was when I was a little boy.

God's promise in my patriarchal blessing sustained me through my mission when other fears surfaced. In France we tracted over eight hours a day, six days a week, for two years!

I never got used to it. I hate to admit it, but I was always a bit relieved when no one was home. God forgive me for this. Those words from my patriarchal blessing were the most important ten-piece promise in my life. Again and again I struggled to believe them and act on them even when my own trembling heart brought evidence against me.

"Seek and Find Thy Helpmate"

I went to Brigham Young University and majored in English, another legacy from Miss Woodward. I knew it was time to think about finding someone to marry, but the last date I went on before my mission as a freshman at BYU, I was so terrified at asking a girl that my roommates dialed the number, handed me the phone, and said, "Talk!" I had dated only once in high school, a close friend, just to get it over with. Otherwise I was too afraid to ask anyone out. I had earned the nickname of "the frog" because I had never kissed a princess. Two years in the mission field without dating was to me a reprieve, not a sacrifice. But I would read my patriarchal blessing and its promise and could bring into my mind the image of the beautiful girl. My mission gave me a little more self-confidence, so I began the courting process. Then I saw Laurie! She was everything I had imagined I wanted in the woman I would marry. I really did have a mental list and she fit every single thing on it, so, of course, it couldn't be true. I was the frog, remember. I was afraid to even dare. She was the girl beyond my dreams. One Sunday she rose to bear her testimony. As she spoke, the words of my patriarchal blessing clearly came into my mind, "likewise pure, clean, and undefiled." I do not believe the Lord was telling me to marry this young woman or that everything would work out if I tried. He is not a *yenta*. But I felt he was telling me to not be afraid, that I could act without fear. The ten pieces were in my hand. The feeling of confidence was so great at that moment that I turned to my roommate and said, "Walter, I'm going to marry that girl." Two months later we were engaged. She married me in spite of all the bungling folly of my courtship. She remains in my memory, even as I write, the girl beyond reality. I have the utmost faith in ten-piece promises, but they do sometimes demand that we reach beyond the earthly evidence that tells us otherwise. We have to live the "if." Yet as we feel after our Father in Heaven, he will provide experiences to strengthen our belief, experiences where we can slide the rent bits of cloth across our hands and believe again, and again, and again, until fulfillment comes.

CHAPTER FOUR

REACHING THROUGH ACTING

*Wherefore, the Lord God gave unto man
that he should act for himself.*

—2 NEPHI 2:16

The Release

Ten-piece wrestling is only one example of reaching for the faith to believe the very truths God has told us. At times, we may be reaching to grasp the strength to act as well as to believe. We want to believe. We do believe—there is no "help thou mine unbelief" (Mark 9:24). Yet acting on God's directions sometimes demands its own form of reaching.

When Laurie and I were the new parents of three small children, we faced a minor crisis of sorts. I was in the early years of my teaching career and fighting to stay on top of the daily demands of a heavy teaching load. I faced what I called the lesson monster. I would spend hours crafting a lesson that would hold the attention of teenagers, teach it, and then have to start all over again, every day, five days a week, for ten months. At the end of each day's instruction, the monster would have eaten my lesson, and he was never satisfied. I also served in several Church callings that demanded my time. Laurie was trying to care for three small children at home. In addition, she was the Young Women's president with a stressful schedule and a large number of girls in the ward.

We seemed to be ships passing in the night. I could feel the pressure pulling on our relationship. Balancing many righteous desires and their demands on our time and energy is its own type of feeling and finding. One afternoon when I was particularly distressed and conflicted, I went down to the river near our house and did a bit of pouring out, mostly of my frustrations. I felt uneasy about the direction our lives were going, and so I wrestled.

In time I felt a very clear answer come to me, but it was not what I expected. "Speak with the bishop and have your wife released," was the counsel I received from the Spirit. I don't know if you have ever argued with the Lord, but I have—on a number of occasions. This was one of them. "You don't ask to be released," I countered. My wife loved her calling; she found validation in it. I was the last person on earth who wanted to tell her she should be released. This got me nowhere as the impression remained. "Please, will you tell her? I can't do it," I offered. But the reply returned was, "She's not asking—you are." Had the spiritual intuition been less clear or one I felt I might have come up with myself, I would have dismissed this prompting, but I was pretty certain the thoughts were not mine. It is one of the ways I know when ideas are the Lord's rather than my own mind speaking— they aren't something I would have come up with on my own. I then felt the Spirit encourage me with a rather blunt truth. "If you are not going to follow my counsels, why do you ask for them?" God often asks us questions when we go to him with our own.

With a very heavy heart, I walked home while the wrestling continued. I could not do this. How would Laurie react? I would have much preferred to be released and allow her to maintain her beloved calling. "Is this a test, Lord?" I asked, then answered my own question. It was not really a test, but a constant opportunity to learn about life and oneself. I've never liked the idea that mortality is just a test. When I reached home, the darkness of my mood and the fear of approaching my wife became almost unbearable. Now you would think that this was not that great of a trial, but we were still in the beginning of discovering one another. I wanted to believe that the course suggested to me was not the right course. I would have never directly opened my innermost thoughts to the Lord at this stage of my life (that would have been a pouring out I was not prepared for), but in reality I was saying, "You're probably right, Lord. But I don't want to do it. Can I have another suggestion?" Does God give suggestions? Or does he only deal in commandments?

I was frightened by the possibilities that this counsel might set in motion. Who was I to expect this of her? Laurie was a very righteous woman, but she did have a strong mind and will of her own. As I turned the doorknob, I received one last impression, that oh-so-near mental voice by which the Lord communicates with us. It was a truth that would help me for the rest of my life in every reaching, every future wrestle, a critical step in feeling after and finding my Father in Heaven. Perhaps the Lord was releasing my wife from her calling simply to teach us this life-enhancing support. "I love your wife more than you do," the inner voice said. "Do you really think I would ever counsel anything that would not be for her benefit?" Knowing this, I could act. Many times our heavenly reaches are answered by a returning question. When we find the reply, we have ended our own dilemmas; the wrestling and feeling after is over. I thought of the testimony of Nephi when he wrote, "He doeth not anything save it be for the benefit of the world; for he loveth the world" (2 Nephi 26:24).

The ensuing conversation with my wife was a difficult one and caused her own reaching, but she accepted the counsel and we went together to the bishop, who was an understanding leader, and the sought-after release was granted. Our lives smoothed out and our ships seemed headed in the same direction again. A few years later, when we moved to another state, Laurie was again called to be the Young Women's president. This time the pressures on our life were different and she served for years. When we moved again six years later, Laurie was called as the Young Women's president and once again served for years in our new ward. A final move to our present stake found her called as the stake Young Women's president. After a few years, she said teasingly to me one day, "You can tell the Lord that he's made it up to me. I wouldn't mind working in the Primary or Relief Society."

"THE WORDS I SHALL SPEAK"

I turn frequently to several critical stories in the scriptures to find help in my face-to-face reaching. The Joseph

Smith story, the story of Enos, and the story of the brother of Jared are among my favorites. They seem to contain a wealth of truth. The combination of these three stories contains such wisdom; I have thought about them and searched them a great deal. When Moriancumer, the brother of Jared, brought his sixteen pure stones to the Lord to have them touched and shine in the darkness of the vessels, a remarkable exchange took place. He prayed, "I know, O Lord, that thou hast all power, and can do whatsoever thou wilt for the benefit of man" (Ether 3:4). Notice that Moriancumer doesn't say that God can do whatever he *wants*; rather, he has power to do whatever he *wills* "for the *benefit* of man." There is, in a way of speaking, a restraining force in God's relationship with his children. He will only do what benefits them. This is what he was telling me as I stood on the doorstep wrestling with his counsels and trying to find the courage to act on that inspiration while at the same time trying to believe they were not the right course to pursue. It is critically important for us in our reaching that we realize and hold this truth in the very core of our souls. Later in the exchanges between Moriancumer and God we learn another oh-so-necessary truth about our relationship with Deity.

Moriancumer saw the finger of the Lord as he reached out to touch the stones. This revelation not only amazes but somewhat shocks Moriancumer and he shrinks from the sight, "fear[ing] lest he should smite me" (Ether 3:8). He did not know the Lord had a body much like his own. Then, from one point of view, the Lord asks a very puzzling question.

"Sawest thou more than this?" (Ether 3:9). Is the Lord really surprised that this mortal has seen his finger? Does he think, *Heavens, he saw my finger; I thought the cloud cover was better*? No. He knows. The question is to draw from Moriancumer a desire to see more. It is a hint; the Lord's hints are always an invitation for reaching. The Lord is usually interested in giving us more than we asked for. Examples of this are myriad. Nephi wanted to see what his father, Lehi, saw in his dream of the tree of life. He was given that and much, much more. Joseph Smith wanted to know which church to join. He was given directions and "many other things did he say unto me, which I cannot write at this time" (JS–H 1:20). Eighteen years after the fact and Joseph still couldn't tell everything he learned at the First Vision.

The brother of Jared took the hint. "And he answered: Nay; Lord, show thyself unto me" (Ether 3:10). That is a bold request, but one the Lord wanted him to make. Then the critical question came, a turning point for Moriancumer: "And the Lord said unto him: Believest thou the words which I shall speak?" (Ether 3:11). Notice the two tenses in that question. *Believest* can be read as past or present tense and is linked in the same sentence with the future tense, *shall speak*. Before we even begin, do you believe what I will say—not *will* you believe, but *do* you? That question carries the implication that acting on the belief will be required. This reaching lifts one right into the presence of God. I fear far too often in my own life I answer the question with, "Well, I would like to hear what you will say and then I'll decide what to think and whether I will act." Do you accept it before I say it?

Moriancumer responds with yet another center-of-the-universe truth about God, equally powerful as knowing he only benefits his children. "Yea, Lord, I know that thou speakest the truth, for thou art a God of truth, and canst not lie" (Ether 3:12). What follows is a revelatory experience beyond the highest expectations Moriancumer could have ever brought as a request to God. He received answers to questions he had never asked. That is what God does. At times, even when we ask wrong or irrelevant questions, he responds with, "Well, here are the answers to the questions you should have asked." God spoke the truth on that afternoon by the river and at the door, and he anticipated that I would respond by acting. But even though I knew in my head his counsel was correct, in my heart there remained a wrestle and a reaching, and I had to decide to act on that knowledge.

I think that sometimes our highest reaching is contained in how we respond to a question God might ask us about our petitions. "If I answer, will you act? Will you believe? Will you testify? Will you live it?" Joseph Smith said, "For how to act I did not know, and unless I could get more wisdom than I then had, I would never know" (JS–H 1:12). God knew this boy. He knew he would believe, and act, and testify. Like Paul before Agrippa, "all the world could not make him think or believe otherwise" (JS–H 1:24). He would act in the face "of the most bitter persecution and reviling" (JS–H 1:23). Joseph wrote later of those persecutions and used two wonderfully powerful words that I have often reflected upon to assess my own commitment to act. "I continued to *affirm* that I had seen a vision" (JS–H 1:27; emphasis added). It was "owing to my continuing to *assert* that I had seen a vision" that stymied his desire to marry Emma Hale and created "the necessity of taking her elsewhere" (JS–H 1:58; emphasis added). Affirm! Assert! Act! I call them the "Three *A*s of Feeling After." Nobody did them better than Joseph Smith. It is not surprising he had so many face-to-face moments with his Father in Heaven.

Oliver Cowdery wanted reassuring confirmations in his life, just as we all do. "I have manifested unto you, by my Spirit in many instances, that the things which you have written are true; wherefore you know that they are true. And if you know that they are true, behold, I give unto you a commandment, that you *rely upon the things* which are written" (D&C 18:2–3; emphasis added). I believe that our reaching consists in these powerful words: *act, affirm, assert, rely.* We could add *testify.* We make sure that the Lord knows, and that *we* know down in our core, that we will put into motion those things he manifests to us; many times we must know this before the manifestation begins.

I spoke earlier of my latest wrestle with faith. When I face dark thoughts that I have lost my Laurie forever, that our covenants in the Lord's House will not be enough, that my failings are too much for even the Savior's vast, boundless mercy and the door to his celestial mansions will be closed to me with her inside—when I pour it all out and reach for assurance and wrestle for faith, I remind myself over and over again, God is a God of truth and does not lie. "Hold on thy way" (D&C 122:9); "All is well! All is well!" (Clayton, *Hymns*, no. 30). I must believe him. I do believe him. I must affirm, assert, and act on those beliefs. I must rely on their truthfulness. Then relief comes, and tears flow, and assurances never asked for descend and settle in, for our Father is a Father of ceaseless, infinite understanding. Yet he is also a God who asks for the past tense of belief and an assurance to act even before the future tense of revealed truth. It is a reaching high enough for heaven.

CHAPTER FIVE

REACHING THROUGH DESIRE

I will sing unto the Lord as long as I live:
I will sing praise to my God while I have my being.
My meditation of him shall be sweet:
I will be glad in the Lord.

—PSALM 104:33–34

"The Motion of a Hidden Fire"

There is a word that commonly appears in verses or stories that deal with prayer. That word is *desire*. Do we not sing, "Prayer is the soul's sincere desire"? (Montgomery, *Hymns*, no. 145). Earlier in my life I might have stopped quoting the hymn there, perhaps because it is the hymn's title. I would talk about the word *desire* and its strong link to prayer. As we do when we pour out, we need to tell the Father our desires. I am almost always asking the question, "God, what desirest thou of me?" It is a welcoming and humbling realization to comprehend how often the question is reversed. This was the earlier limit of my understanding. Desire always meant a request either from me or from the Lord. Jesus, remember, was always most concerned with knowing what people desired of him, even to the point of asking his disciples what they wanted him to do for them when he returned to his Father.

Now, however, I remind myself to continue the hymn to include the rest of the stanza, "uttered or *unexpressed*, / the *motion* of a hidden fire / That *trembles* in the breast" (*Hymns*,

107

no. 145; emphasis added). It is the unexpressed portion, the motion, the trembling I would like to explore—those things not requested, but felt deep in the soul. These are poetic phrases, I acknowledge, but they describe a reaching and feeling after that does not rely on words; this is often a difficult reaching to attain. It may not be so much a face-to-face conversation, but a soul-to-soul sharing. The mind is always busy, wishing to speak, but the soul may need quiet, wanting to feel. Most of our reaching will probably be of the uttered kind, but there is an equal potential in the unexpressed kind. In fact it may be a higher reaching. Here *desire* may not mean those things I want or need, but simply love. For example, as I think of my wife, who recently passed away, I am filled with desire. This means, certainly, I would love to be with her, to talk with her, but it implies at its purest and highest level that the thought of her fills me with love. That love carries naturally within it the desire to be a better person, one of the truest qualities of love. So it is with God. Being filled with desire of this type lifts one to want intensely to live in such a manner that the Father would say of us, "This is my dear child, in whom I delight."

We might remember that Jesus introduced the Lord's Prayer with the words, "Your Father knoweth what things ye have need of, before ye ask him" (Matthew 6:8). This was itself preceded by the counsel not to pray as the heathen do who "think that they shall be heard for their much speaking" (Matthew 6:7). Both phrases suggest little speaking because it may not be necessary.

When Joseph Smith went into the Sacred Grove, he "kneeled down and began to offer up the desires of [his] heart to God" (JS–H 1:15). I assume that his earnest search included both words and thoughts and that they were specific; God does like specific praying. This seems to have been an uttered reaching. When the brother of Jared brought his sixteen stones to God, he reminded the Lord that men had been given "a commandment that we must call upon thee, that from thee we may receive according to our desires" (Ether 3:2). Once again I assume the usage of *desire* here refers to requests—the uttered prayer. But when, by contrast, the word *desire* is used in 3 Nephi 19 in describing the disciples, I sense we may be dealing with what has been called the "Prayer of Quiet." In 3 Nephi we read, "They did not multiply many words, for it was given unto them what they should pray, and they were filled with desire" (3 Nephi 19:24). *Desire* here seems to mean emotion, feeling, love, adoration, and unity rather than requests. And those feelings generate a need to sanctify oneself to become more pleasing to the beloved.

In my interactions with Laurie, I was always too full of words. I wanted to express them, but often silence was the greater demonstration of love and the most needful, or the most unifying, or the most healing. If I could just still my urge to talk! I failed so often at this that it was almost habitual. I could almost overcome this habit with my children—at least I succeeded more often. I could hold them on my lap in a rocking chair and quietly rock back and forth. It was the love we both felt that was most critical. To this day, my oldest daughter talks of quiet times rocking in the chair as some of her fondest memories of growing up.

THE PRAYER OF QUIET

Perhaps we can illustrate with the help of a famous Catholic saint. During the sixteenth century, Spain produced a number of remarkable people who taught a more personal approach to God than the formal ritual associated with Catholic worship. Saint Teresa of Ávila was one of them. She tried to guide others into a more meaningful relationship with God, one centered on love, on "being filled with desire." This, she believed, would invite people to live higher lives.

Teresa spoke of the soul as a garden that needed watering; the water could be supplied in different ways. In the garden grew the flowers, shrubs, and trees of human virtues. Each soul would want his or her garden to be beautiful so the Lord would walk in it. "With God's help, we have to make these plants grow, as good gardeners do," she wrote, "watering them carefully so that they don't die but begin producing flowers, which give off an appealing scent, to delight this Lord of ours. Then He will come frequently to . . . take pleasure in these virtues." This metaphor gave Teresa a great deal of comfort and helped her convey her own experiences to others. "It used to please me enormously to think of my soul as a garden, and imagine that the Lord was walking in it. I begged Him to increase the fragrance of those little flowers of virtue that were, it seemed, just starting to bloom. . . . *I didn't want anything for myself"* (Medwick, *Teresa of Avila*, 99, 104; emphasis added).

For Teresa, desire meant love, not requests. Prayer was the primary source of water, but the word *prayer* is in some ways insufficient. The garden could be irrigated by drawing from a well. More efficient ways were possible, however. We all know rain is more effective in watering plants than pumping from a well or diverting streams. Drawing water from the well, generally speaking, is what we have been calling reaching for God. Rain is God pouring his love into our souls, teaching us what to feel and ask and nourishing our growing virtues. Both are necessary.

Many only pray with the head, what Teresa called the Prayer of Recollection, but the more spiritually mature learn to reach out with their hearts and attain the Prayer of Quiet. In the Prayer of Recollection, the memory and mind are very active, searching for things for which to thank God or expressing our needs and desires as requests. We are the main irrigators in the Prayer of Recollection, but in the Prayer of Quiet, the mind calms, the always-probing memory is stilled, desire fills the soul, and the rain falls. Obviously we do not control the rain—it is God's grace to us—but it comes because we yearn for it.

When God's love does the watering, we need to eliminate the noise. "What I call noise is scurrying around with the intellect to come up with lots of words and thoughts to use in thanking God for this blessing, and piling up sins and faults to make it obvious that these gifts are undeserved. Everything is in motion, the intellect showing what it can do, and the memory rushing about" (Medwick, *Teresa of Avila*, 105). I remember the first time I read these words. They struck me as powerfully as scripture. What Teresa described is what I do frequently. I realized that often when I become aware of God's love or of his presence drawing near, I feel a great need to talk to him, to pour out. Yet many times, I could, if I allowed it, sense the Lord saying to me: *Mike, you don't need to say anything. You don't need to thank me. Let's just walk together for a while and share one another's love.* Sometimes—not often enough—we simply wish to say, "I love thee, Father, and I love thy Son." Nothing else is necessary.

I return to Teresa's attempts to explain her Prayer of Quiet or what I call reaching and feeling after through desire. As she indicates, there is a tremendous peace that accompanies the Prayer of Quiet. We cannot enter into this peace at will. I'm afraid if it was always available, I would be constantly saying, "Again, Lord, again." But that peace can come into our lives sufficiently to inspire sanctification and help us to say in part, as Jesus did in whole, "I and my Father are one" (John 10:30). Did not Jesus fervently beseech God that all those who believed in him might enjoy that same oneness? (see John 17; 3 Nephi 19).

The Prayer of Quiet we speak of "is a state in which the soul enters into peace," Teresa writes, "or rather in which the Lord gives it peace through His presence. . . . In this state all the faculties are stilled. The soul . . . realizes that it is now very close to its God, and that, if it were but a little closer, it would become one with Him through union. . . .

"The soul is conscious of a deep satisfaction. So glad is it merely to find itself near the fountain that, even before it has begun to drink, it has had its fill. *There seems nothing left for it to desire.* . . . The mind tries to occupy itself with only one thing, and the memory has no desire to busy itself with more: they both see that this is the one thing needful. . . . *They are so overwhelmed and absorbed by the joy and delight which they experience that they can think of nothing to ask for,* and will gladly say with Saint Peter: 'Lord, let us make here three mansions'" (St. Teresa, *The Way of Perfection*, 200–202; emphasis added).

Though our Father in Heaven gives this rain, we can still open ourselves to it. We can turn up the soil of our hearts and minds to allow the water to penetrate root-deep. As this is the Prayer of Quiet, quiet places with room for reflection and pondering are essential: "It is well to seek greater solitude so as to make room for the Lord and allow His Majesty to do His own work in us. . . .

"There are persons—and I have been one of them—to whom the Lord gives tenderness of devotion and holy inspirations and light on everything. He bestows this Kingdom on them and brings them to this Prayer of Quiet, and yet they deafen their ears to His voice. For they are so fond of talking and of repeating a large number of vocal prayers in a great hurry, as though they were anxious to finish their task of repeating them daily, that when the Lord, as I say, puts His kingdom into their very hands, *by giving them this Prayer of Quiet and this inward peace*, they do not accept it, but think they will do better to go on reciting their prayers, which only distracts them from their purpose. . . .

"He to Whom you are praying is very near to you and will not fail to hear you; and you may be sure that you are truly praising Him and hallowing His name, since you are glorifying the Lord as a member of His household and *praising Him with increasing affection and desire so that it seems you can never forsake His service*" (Saint Teresa, *The Way of Perfection*, 204, 209; emphasis added).

"GIVEN UNTO THEM WHAT THEY SHOULD PRAY"

There is another element inherent in reaching through desire that we see describe the disciples in 3 Nephi 19. Here we read that intriguing line, "It was given unto them what they should pray" (3 Nephi 19:24). This same truth is repeated in Doctrine and Covenants 50, "But know this, it shall be given you what you shall ask" (D&C 50:30). Perhaps *desire*, with these verses in mind, may mean we are so united in oneness with the Father that our hearts, minds, and wills are the same. We think, feel, love, share, request—the very things God wishes for us to have or do because of this oneness. We draw closer to the relationship that Christ enjoyed with his Father, wherein he often said, "I and my Father are one." I believe we witness this type of being filled with desire in the great vision Enoch received as recorded in Moses 7. This is one of the most magnificently beautiful experiences offered by the scriptures. I never read it without my faith in Joseph Smith's prophetic calling being renewed to affirmation if not certitude.

Enoch watches as God weeps over the "residue" of people left after Zion has been translated into the peace of God's presence. These are the wicked, yet God weeps with profound sorrow over their sufferings. As the vision continues, Enoch seeks to understand the mind and heart of God and his reason for such grief. "These are my creations, my children," the Lord explains. "They are suffering. They are miserable and I so wanted them to be happy; to love each other and choose me as their Father. In time all the heavens and all their inhabitants will weep as they see the sufferings of men." When this understanding is reached—when it penetrates to Enoch's core, he becomes one, heart and mind, with his Creator. God fills him with the desire of an Eternal Father for his children in their sufferings. It is one of the most powerful face-to-face moments in sacred writ. My most beloved verse of all scripture follows: "And it came to pass that the Lord spake unto Enoch, and told Enoch all the doings of the children of men; wherefore Enoch knew, and looked upon their wickedness, and their misery, and wept and stretched forth his arms, and his heart swelled wide as eternity; and his bowels yearned; and all eternity shook" (Moses 7:41). *Shook* in this context means to overflow. All eternity overflows with compassion, mercy, and love. There is not space enough to contain it.

Enoch is filled with desire, the desire of God. I believe this is exactly what God wanted Enoch to feel at this moment in his life. I believe it is what he wants all of us to feel.

What we call *charity* in Christianity is the highest of all virtues—higher even than faith itself. Too many Christians have forgotten this, engaging in endless debates about doctrinal issues over the centuries. There are few arguments over the prodigal son, the good Samaritan, or the washing of feet. If faith is essential in our feeling after and finding God, how much more essential is the quality of charity that Enoch so profoundly received? In that Himalayan peak of Christian scripture, 1 Corinthians 13, Paul gives a magnificent description of charity and ends with this conclusion: "And now abideth faith, hope, charity, these three; *but the greatest of these is charity*" (1 Corinthians 13:13; emphasis added). It is the most appealing of all desires. Mormon testified to its necessity also, reminding us that charity "endureth forever; and whoso is found possessed of it at the last day, it shall be well with him" (Moroni 7:47). What more pleasing face-to-face meeting could God find acceptable than when our love mirrors his own, and his desires become our desires? We love him, certainly, but we also love those he loves. Our love for him, as Teresa of Ávila knew, brings him into our gardens. Our love for our fellowmen is a reaching just as high. It may even be the supreme reaching, the most beautiful of feeling afters.

Let us return to the idea that when we are reaching with desire we are often inspired about what to pray for, that our hearts and minds may be one with our Father. An illustration may be helpful. When I was younger, I was quite troubled with the teaching that little children who die "before they arrive at the years of accountability are saved in the celestial kingdom of heaven" (D&C 137:10). It seemed to me as if they were being given a free pass. I do not wish to sound uncharitable; I was happy with God's mercy for his little children. I didn't want to change the doctrine. I loved the idea; I just wanted to be the recipient of it. I often said, "I should have died when I was seven." Rather than being grateful to have been born in such a wonderful time and place, I thought it would have been better to have been born in a very poor country in an age in which most children did not survive. "The celestial kingdom will be full of these children," I thought.

I wrestled with this doctrine for years. How was it just? How did it unite with the other spokes in the wheel of scripture which talked of righteousness, diligence, and obedience? For billions of souls, life was not a test, just a matter of getting out before you messed everything up with the ill-use of agency. I believed that the critical factor for celestial glory wasn't good deeds, words, thoughts, or attitudes accumulated throughout life, but the absence of their opposites. It seemed to me that staying pure was the key and that children had the best chance at maintaining this state. Why hadn't I died early?

I was able for a long time to put the question to rest by the thought that this teaching was not in the scriptures, but in the non-canonical teachings of Joseph Smith. While those teachings are something we certainly shouldn't ignore, there was some room for discussion or debate. This seemed to bring it down a few rungs on the doctrinal ladder. I could, as is said, put it on the shelf. All this changed when the revelations we recognize as sections 137 and 138 were canonized in the April 1976 general conference (originally included in the Pearl of Great Price, they were added to the Doctrine and Covenants as sections 137 and 138 in 1979). When it *was* in the scriptures, my dilemma returned full-force. I was well into adulthood and had made sufficient mistakes, broken enough commandments, and accumulated adequate guilt to intensify my disappointment at not having died when I was seven.

While serving a mission in France, I had an interview with Elder Marion G. Romney. At the end of his questions, he graciously asked me if I had any question I would like to ask an apostle. I am sure he was hoping I had the good sense to say no, realizing he had more than a hundred interviews to conduct. Here was my opportunity. I could not just let it slip away over polite protocol. So I said, "I do have one thing that has troubled me for a long time. Why is it fair that little children go to the celestial kingdom by simply dying young? I should have died when I was seven. Then eternity for me would have been assured." He smiled as if he had heard this query a hundred times, reached out and patted my knee reassuringly, and said, "Now don't you worry, elder, everyone who goes to the celestial kingdom will deserve to be there." I thanked him and left, still puzzled and thinking, *That was no answer at all, but then, I suppose there isn't an answer that will ever put it to rest.*

This wrestle continued on in my life until one day, when

I was preparing a lesson about the disciples in 3 Nephi not multiplying many words, but being filled with desire and having the Spirit tell them what to offer God. In a pure moment of self-awareness, I realized I had never purposefully prayed that way. This revealed truth didn't make me despair, but it did embarrass me. How could I have missed this? I thought about it a great deal, and while driving home one afternoon, I prayed, "Father in Heaven, if there is anything I should pray for, anything you would have me desire, if you will tell me, I will pray for it. I will try to put it into my heart and mind. I will try to make thy thoughts my own." Sometimes we ask the right things and the answers come quickly. It feels as if God is saying to us, *I have been waiting some time for you to come to me with this. Now you are here. We can talk and you can learn.* Sometimes it doesn't even matter what the question is. Our intense hunger to know something—anything—from the Lord creates a space for insight. The Lord says to us, *That was a good question. Your desire for wisdom is received and acknowledged. However, I will give you the answer to the question you should have asked.*

When I approached God with that mixture of question and commitment, my mind filled with words, my heart flowed with emotion, and I offered them all to God. *Thank your Father,* the Spirit instructed, *that you did not die when you were seven. And plead earnestly that you might live for a very, very long time that you will be able to gather all the wonderful lessons and truths that life's experiences will teach you—which you cannot acquire any other way.* I was filled with desire, with an intense love of God. I didn't need to say a single thing. Life was a dear and lovely thing and it was mine to enjoy. I was immersed in gratitude for the seasons of my life, those that had passed and those that yet awaited me. I suppose God could have told me that sooner, but I wonder if it would have had as much impact when I was younger and had not yet tasted the beauty of living and learning on this imperfect but lovely earth. Perhaps of all the thoughts and feelings I have ever offered up to God, those at that hour were the most proper because God gave them to me: they came from the heart and mind of God himself. I recall to this day those feelings, the love that accompanied them, and the very spot when they were given to me. Every time I drive by that spot I remember, and life again is full and joyous, a thing of wonder, something to be treasured with each drawing breath.

"WITH GRACE IN YOUR HEARTS"

The Apostle Paul knew and testified to the power of reaching with desire and being helped to do so by heaven's grace. He did not speak a great deal about it; it is so very difficult to describe, though many have tried as Saint Teresa did. It is something we experience. My efforts in trying to delineate its boundaries will, of necessity, fall short. Paul described it as well as one can in a brief simple statement in Romans: "The Spirit also *helpeth* our infirmities: for we know not what we should pray for as we ought: but *the Spirit itself maketh intercession for us with groanings which cannot be uttered*" (Romans 8:26; emphasis added). We see again the idea of unuttered communication. Perhaps the hymn writer was thinking of Paul's words when he penned, "Prayer is the soul's sincere desire, / Uttered or unexpressed" (Montgomery, *Hymns*, no. 145).

Paul linked these unuttered prayers with the mind and will of God. Notice the use of those two words in the following verse. "And he that *searcheth the hearts* knoweth what is the *mind of the Spirit*, because he maketh intercession for the saints according to *the will of God*" (Romans 8:27; emphasis added). *Heart*, *mind*, and *will* are all used in this verse. All are one—our hearts, the Spirit's mind, and the will of God. All speak with the same voice. It is the voice of our Father, true, but it is equally our own voice. I think of the story my mother told me as a child about an elephant and a mouse that crossed a bridge together. As they walked, the bridge trembled, shook, and echoed thunder with their passing. At the far side, the mouse looked up, beaming with joy and excitement. "Didn't we make that bridge sing!" he said, and the elephant only smiled and nodded. This is Teresa's Prayer of Quiet *and* those deeper prayers, when God sends the rain to our roots. The Spirit reaches down and draws water for us, or rain falls upon our souls and the flowers of faith, devotion, obedience, virtue, courage, adoration, gratitude—and especially love—spring up. God can walk with us in our garden, one that he himself is primarily responsible for having created. But we both are fulfilled, both satisfied with a mutual giving and receiving.

One final thought may be helpful. Music is a great aid in this type of reaching, as are the quiet beautiful solitudes of nature. There are times, I'm sure, in all our lives when we are so moved by a piece of music or magnificent landscape that no words are necessary. The soul just fills with desire. I have felt this way when hearing "O Divine Redeemer," "Come, Thou Fount of Every Blessing," "O Come, O Come, Emmanuel," or "Goin' Home." We receive a special holiness of joy each Christmas season with carol singing that often takes us to Bethlehem on that holy night two thousand years ago. We mingle our own voices with the "multitude of the heavenly host praising God, and saying, Glory to God in the highest" (Luke 2:13–14). Paul taught this to the early Saints in more than one epistle. To the Ephesians he wrote, "Be filled with the Spirit; *speaking to yourselves* in psalms and hymns and spiritual songs, singing and making melody in your heart to the Lord" (Ephesians 5:18–19; emphasis added). Should we read the phrase *speaking to yourselves* as plural or singular? Are we speaking to each other in the congregation, or having an internal dialogue with God in the silent hollows of our souls? It can certainly be both.

I recall a moment when I was a small child of maybe seven or eight hearing my mother singing "More Holiness Give Me." She had a beautiful trained singing voice, and as I listened, two lines of the hymn in particular caused, to use Enos's words, "the joy . . . [to sink] deep into my heart. And my soul hungered" (Enos 1:3–4). These are the lines: "More longing for home," and "More, Savior, like thee" (Bliss,

Hymns, no. 131). Those words filled me with desire. I was overwhelmed with a sense of divine homesickness and love. I knew this world was not my home, but that my home was with my Father in Heaven. I wanted desperately to return. I believed that he loves me. I also knew that the road of my returning was to be more like my Savior. We went home from that sacrament meeting and I climbed a tree in the front yard so I could be alone. The leaves closed around me and I sang that hymn over and over to myself. Perhaps this is what Paul was suggesting; I was being guided and taught by the Spirit, even as a child, how to make "melody in your heart to the Lord" (Ephesians 5:19).

Paul wrote similar counsel to the Colossians but with slightly different words. It is helpful to look at the difference. Paul spoke again of "psalms and hymns and spiritual songs," but this time, instead of "melody in the heart," he said, "singing with *grace in your hearts* to the Lord" (Colossians 3:16; emphasis added). The reaching with desire, as we have seen, is accomplished only through the grace of God. It is partially a gift, an intercession—God coming to us. We sing in another hymn, "He answers privately, / Reaches my reaching" (Thayne, *Hymns*, no. 129). We sing with grace in our hearts, giving back the gift even as it is bestowed.

We also have the Lord's words to Emma Smith regarding music as a help in having our voices reach to the heavens. In Doctrine and Covenants 25, the union of prayer and song is plain; it gives pleasure to God as well as ourselves: "For *my soul delighteth in the song of the heart*; yea, the song of the righteous *is a prayer* unto me, and it shall be answered with a blessing upon their heads" (v. 12; emphasis added). Sometimes when I feel the power of music, be it the words or the melody, I wonder: *Is the song drawing out of me the emotions, thoughts, love, gratitude that are already there, but expressed in a way beyond my own talents—or is it putting them into me as a free gift of the Spirit?* I suppose it is both. Either way, music is a great facilitator for the Prayer of Quiet, the reaching through desire.

We live in such a bustling world of noise, where everyone and everything seems to be in constant motion. It becomes increasingly difficult to access this particular feeling after and finding God, yet it may be one of the most necessary. Quieting our surroundings must certainly precede calming the soul and tuning the spiritual ear. It is a way of inviting our Father in Heaven into our thoughts and, perhaps even more important, of inviting him into our garden, where his presence nourishes the virtues and allows them to bloom. Perhaps this is the truest meaning of the Father's own words, "Be still, and know that I am God" (Psalm 46:10). Stillness is a necessary prelude to the knowing that comes after. The outward world need not dismay us. There is a calm center. We may enter it when we are filled with desire; for this we are allowed God's intervening grace.

CHAPTER SIX

REACHING THROUGH KNOCKING

The keeper of the gate is the Holy One of Israel;
and he employeth no servant there. . . .
And whoso knocketh, to him will he open.

—2 NEPHI 9:41–42

THE KNOCK OF FAMILIARITY

In the Bible and in the Book of Mormon, Jesus told us that if we knocked, it would be opened unto us (see Matthew 7:7; Luke 11:9; 3 Nephi 14:7). If you close your eyes and picture the door that is to be opened, on which side do you place yourself and on which the Savior? Are you on the outside? Is the Savior? If we think carefully we can see that what is critical is not whose door it is, but if we are familiar with the voice on the other side. If I were to arrive at home and knock at the front door for admission, my wife or children might call out: "Who is it?" With a simple two-syllable answer, I can gain entrance. I would say, "It's me!" How interesting! The human voice is so unique that among the billions of humans on the earth, my own particular voice would be recognized. And why? Because the person on the other side of the door has heard it many, many times and is familiar with it. When we talk about reaching through knocking, we are, in a sense, reaching with our past reachings. Let's see how this works with a few scriptures.

The parable of the ten virgins is a good place to start.

Laying aside the usual focus on having our lamps filled with oil, we move to the scene where the five foolish virgins arrive at the wedding. Here is the door and they knock. Jesus, the bridegroom, is on the inside. "Afterward came also the other virgins, saying, Lord, Lord, open to us. But he answered and said, Verily I say unto you, I know you not" (Matthew 25:11–12). I'm not convinced that this rejection is only because they are unprepared. I think it may also be because they are not familiar. The bridegroom does not know their voices. Why would he not know their voices? Because he has not heard them before—at least not frequently enough to allow entrance. In those circumstances, "I know you not" is much less harsh an answer. In this light we might also read Jesus' comments in the Sermon on the Mount wherein he says, "And then will I profess unto them, I never knew you" (Matthew 7:23). Sometimes this is rendered, "You never knew me." However you want to read this statement, it suggests the actions and works of the individual have not allowed the close understanding that comes with frequent conversations and unity of purpose. There have been few, if any, past face-to-face conversations.

If we shift to the gospel of Luke, we see a much shorter parable, but one that draws upon the same ideas. Guests are assembling for a wedding. "Let your loins be girded about, and your lights burning; and ye yourselves like unto men that wait for their lord, when he will return from the wedding; that when he cometh and knocketh, they may *open unto him immediately*" (Luke 12:35–36; emphasis added). Notice that in Luke, the bridegroom is outside the door and knocking. We must read a bit between the lines, but the word *immediately* can imply several things. They open right away because they expect him. They open without delay because the house is tidy and clean. They don't need to cry out, "Just a minute!" and shove the dirty socks under the couch. However, they also open instantly because they recognize the voice from the other side. "That is my master! That is my Lord! I know that voice. I have heard it many times and I always respond." The beauty in Luke's account is that when entry is granted, the Lord himself serves the supper. That is humility high as the heavens. This is a supper of truth, knowledge, love, and friendship. We feast on eternal sustenance, with Christ as the preparer and as the one who serves the meal. (See Luke 12:37.) It is easy to see how the knocking of familiarity dovetails so well with reaching with desire and the Prayer of Quiet. We know each other; the love is already established.

This is the power behind the parable of the good shepherd as well. The deeper insight comes not so much from the sheep's willingness to follow, but the reason why they follow. They know their shepherd's voice! They have heard it before. In the parable this is made perfectly clear: "He that entereth in by the door is the shepherd of the sheep. To him the porter openeth; and *the sheep hear his voice*: and he calleth his own sheep by name, and leadeth them out. And when he putteth forth his own sheep, he goeth before them, and the sheep follow him: for *they know his voice*. And a stranger will they not follow . . . for *they know not the voice of strangers*" (John

10:2–5; emphasis added). Once again, it is Christ, our shepherd, on the outside of the door, but his voice is familiar, the door opens, and the sheep follow.

King Benjamin also used the idea of the Savior's voice compared to a stranger's, but told us why and how the voice is known. "I would that ye should remember to retain the name written always in your hearts . . . that ye hear and know the voice by which ye shall be called. . . . For *how knoweth a man the master whom he has not served, and who is a stranger unto him, and is far from the thoughts and intents of his heart?*" (Mosiah 5:12–13; emphasis added). It is all a question of familiarity. The voice on either the inside or the outside of the door must be distinguished, the family member or close friend instantly identified. We know that voice through long association because the Master has always been in the thoughts and intents of our hearts.

When the brother of Jared offered his three pleadings in Ether 1 (that he and his brother's language not be confounded, then that their friends' language not be confounded, and then that the Lord would lead them to a promised land), we are told in all three moments that the Lord answered because he "had compassion" (see Ether 1:35, 37, 40). When reaching toward heaven in any manner, we must constantly remember this! We are speaking with a compassionate being, more compassionate than anyone we have ever met on earth. However, the last verse of Ether 1 adds an important detail. God first grants them blessings they did not ask for—that is so like the Lord—then he gives the "why" of his response. "And thus I will do unto thee because *this long time* ye have cried unto me" (Ether 1:43; emphasis added). Consistently asking and receiving has, over time, acquainted these two beings with each other. Each other's voice and heart are mutually known. When the knock comes from either side, the door opens.

There is one more door we can examine. It is perhaps the most famous door in scripture; there are artistic renditions of this door commonly seen in the Church. It is found in Revelation 3, when John addresses the Saints in Laodicea. "Behold, I stand at the door, and knock: if any man hear my voice, and open the door, I will come in to him, and will sup with him, and he with me" (Revelation 3:20). In this image, God is on the outside and wants entry into our lives. The hope this verse inspires is augmented when we realize the Laodiceans were warned earlier, "Thou art lukewarm, and neither hot nor cold" (Revelation 3:16). Yet even for these half-committed Saints, the Lord knocks, and he offers the promised mutual feasting of truth and goodness. The knocking is accompanied by words. If the Saints will, they can "hear my voice." But they must know that voice and understand what is granted when they swing the door open. We can further enhance the dignity and graciousness of Christ's divine humility—he comes to my door to call and knock—by finding a second door in this chapter. In John's message to the Saints in Philadelphia, we see the door to living with the Savior. Is it open or shut? "I know thy works: behold, I have set before thee an open door, and no man can shut it"

(Revelation 3:8). Things are much better among the Saints in Philadelphia. He knows their works, and we cannot help but conclude that what they have done has contributed to the door before them being open.

As I grow older and experience the wonder of the temple more each year, I am always acutely edified to discover that almost every principle, doctrine, application, law, or tenet of our religion is amplified and demonstrated in the ordinances of the Lord's House. The temple is a microcosm of the broader unity of all we believe and all we attempt to live. If we reflect on everything we do within those sacred walls, we will shortly realize that scriptural teachings about doors and knocking are beautifully presented in that holy house. We cannot help but understand when we leave the temple, after having experienced anew the rejuvenating energy of the endowment, that past faithfulness in all things allows us to anticipate a glorious reception when we approach our Father in Heaven's celestial doors. Having been true to our covenants, and having lived according to what God has already revealed, additional light, truth, wisdom, and knowledge will surely be granted. Conversations with God, through the celestial curtain that has separated us from him during our mortal journey, are the key to our reunion with him for eternity.

The last serene, intimate, warm, and beautifully peaceful conclusion of the endowment is a tranquil, stilling summation of a lifetime of reaching, wrestling, and pouring out, of believing, acting, and knocking. We are being taught the highest way to meet with God face to face. We have, throughout the endowment, been feeling after him. All through the temple ordinances the expectation is that we will surely find him. These truths dovetail in perfect harmony, particularly with our reaching through acting discussed in chapter four. As the spokes of a wheel drawn tightly together by the central pull of the hub, every truth and goodness of the gospel present to us one holistic unity. In the Lord's wisdom, he impelled me to wrestle long to obtain my own personal love of the temple. To my mind, the manner in which the endowment ceremony teaches the Savior's gentle imploring that if we "knock . . . it shall be opened unto you" (Matthew 7:7) is the single most uplifting moment in that sacred building.

PONDERING—THE KNOCK OF INQUIRY

We might also consider that another type of knocking is the approach to the Lord's door we call pondering. We could call this the serene knock of inquiry. Wrestling, which we discussed earlier, is a more vigorous knocking. The knocking of familiarity is developed over time and with a mutual sharing of common purpose and love, of moments spent together in the soul's garden. It is often followed by and demonstrated through actions of obedience and uncommanded goodness. Pondering is more solitary. It is a word we use a great deal. As with the word *prayer*, *pondering* may have been used so much it has begun to lose some of its muscle. Unfortunately, familiarity can slow spiritual energy.

Pondering may be a search for all the possible courses from which we can choose. Then, when we meet with God face to face, we have all our choices before us and can ask for help in moving in the best direction. We have, in a manner of speaking, done our homework. Far too often I want God to go through all the possibilities and pick one for me. We need to do what Moriancumer did and molten out of the rock of our mental labor the white stones we bring to the Lord. Our own white stones may be exactly what God himself would have counseled, or they may be far from the mark, and we will need to return to our places of pondering. God may say to us, "Well, this is not what I would have thought or done, but it is your idea. We will go with it and all will still be well." He is trying to teach us to be Gods, remember, and that will ultimately demand a great deal of independent thought. Learning the pondering process may well be more important than anything that results from it. Sometimes this is a wrestling process, but far more often it involves a meditative mind, which can see potential paths more easily when the soul is tranquil and composed.

Pondering is also a calming of the mind. It is frequently useful for me to use that wonderful gift of human imagination to create mental pictures that help me visualize what I'm trying to do spiritually. My mental image of pondering is the reflection on the surface of a lake. When we lived in Alberta and Colorado, I did a great deal of backpacking. Among the high peaks of the Rocky Mountains there are beautiful lakes with summits soaring around them. In the early morning

I would rise and hike up the slope a few hundred feet and look down on the lake below. There you could see two twin mountain chains, one lifting high above you and one reaching into the dark waters of the lake. The impact is stunning; it would take my breath away. On the surface of the water, which was quiet with velvet smoothness, you could see the mountains mirrored perfectly. Often the smallest details of tree, glacier, and rock could be discerned in the lake's double. However, the slightest ripple would distort the matching image. The more troubled the water, the less one could see. We calm our minds so that reality can be revealed on our minds' mirror, even in the tiniest of detail. We start to learn how to read heaven's will as we might plan the day's route by following a reflected path in a mountain lake. This image has been beneficial to me from time to time.

When we still our minds, thus inviting the Lord's reflections to reveal themselves, we are saying to God, "I am ready to receive." God is a teacher at heart, and every teacher knows that hungry students are practically irresistible. Enos simply said, "My soul hungered" (Enos 1:4). Being prepared to receive, however, sometimes requires a pouring out of anxiety, care, worry, pressure, impatience, and a half-dozen other things that might trouble the water. Harboring these emotions is like throwing rocks into the lake. Our pondering will be largely fruitless if our cares are constant enough to never allow our minds sufficient calm for God to show us truth and goodness.

It takes diligence and practice to learn how to hold our mind centered on one thing or to clear it and wait to see what the Lord may show us on its surface. I have what the Buddha called a monkey mind—thoughts bumping into each other, changing direction, leaping from branch to branch, never staying still, always in motion. Stilling this energetic and wild little animal is a lifetime pursuit. Can one "practice" revelation? Not really, I suppose, but one can develop the presence and control of mind that invites it, or summons it, and then sustains it. One of the reasons that vocal prayer is often so much more effective resides in its ability to help keep our thoughts focused. A world-changing example of the commanding energy of pondering is the moment of enlightenment the Buddha had while he sat, with a stilled and focused mind, under the Bodhi tree seeking an answer to human suffering. During this time, Mara, the Buddhist equivalent of Satan, tried various ways to distract his mental concentration, but he had trained his mind through long years to remain steady and undivided, and in time the great revelation that became the foundation teaching of Buddhism cleared on the surface of his mind's lake.

The Scriptural Catalyst

Through the mental stimulus of pondering, the scriptures can help us focus and create opportunities for us to knock at the Lord's door. Considering the setting we place ourselves in when we ponder may enhance our experience. I think of Joseph Smith in the woods, Nephi or Jesus on the mountaintop, Enos in the woods, or President Kimball "spending many long hours in the Upper Room of the Temple supplicating the Lord for divine guidance" (Official Declaration 2). I have found it helpful while pondering scripture to examine the individual words themselves or the narrative, looking for relevance. Sometimes a single word or a familiar story looked at from a different person's point of view opens up new worlds of truth. The parable of the prodigal son can be read from three points of view: the elder son's, the younger son's, and the father's. When we reflect on each of these three perspectives, they give widening reaches of understanding. A few examples may be useful in illustrating the reaching that pondering scripture can generate.

Notice how President Joseph F. Smith introduces his vision regarding the preaching of the gospel among the departed spirits of earth: "I sat in my room pondering over the scriptures; and reflecting upon the great atoning sacrifice that was made by the Son of God, for the redemption of the world. . . . While I was thus engaged, my mind reverted to the writings of the apostle Peter. . . . I opened the Bible and read. . . . As I pondered over these things which are written, the eyes of my understanding were opened, and the Spirit of the Lord rested upon me, and I saw the hosts of the dead" (D&C 138:1–2, 5–6, 11). The act of pondering scripture was the catalyst that God used to show President Smith the truth of the hereafter.

When Doctrine and Covenants 76 was given to Joseph Smith and Sidney Rigdon, "being in the Spirit . . . by the power of the Spirit our eyes were opened and our understandings were enlightened, so as to see and understand the things of God" (D&C 76:11–12). What was the initial pondering that opened their eyes? "We came to the twenty-ninth verse of the fifth chapter of John. . . . Now *this caused us to marvel*, for it was given unto us of the Spirit" (D&C 76:15, 18; emphasis added). Joseph Smith's entire life was marked by a spirit of inquiry, of pondering deeply, reflecting on matters of cosmic depth. He addressed the First Vision account to "all inquirers after truth" (JS–H 1:1), and set the standard of what such an inquirer would do.

I believe this is the foundational reason that God chose this particular young man to lead the Restoration. He knew Joseph wanted "certain conclusion[s]" (JS–H 1:8) and would not be satisfied with less. He was intense in his desire of "settling the question" (JS–H 1:12). His reading of James 1:5 sent him into the woods after he had "reflected on it again and again" (JS–H 1:12). Earlier in the account of his search, he stated "my mind was called up to *serious reflection* and great uneasiness" (JS–H 1:8; emphasis added). The principle and ordinance of eternal marriage, that central pillar of our mortal and our postmortal happiness, was given because Joseph "inquired . . . to know and understand" why the Lord allowed the biblical patriarchs to have plural wives (D&C 132:1). Though his initial question was not about the everlasting sealing of man and wife, that question prompted the Lord to reveal the "new and everlasting covenant" of marriage (D&C 132:4). In Doctrine and Covenants 132, eternal marriage is the main theme of the revelation; plural marriage is secondary.

Time after time as Joseph searched the scriptures he would ponder, reflect, meditate, consider, theorize, and ask. I also believe this is why the Lord had him work at his translation of the Bible. Correcting or clarifying certain verses was secondary to the main benefit of causing Joseph to inquire. Here we see God's wisdom as he works through his prophets. As stated in *Lectures on Faith*, when reviewing the influence of past generations' testimonies on present ones, "this testimony having *aroused their minds to inquire* after the knowledge of God; the inquiry frequently terminated, indeed always terminated when rightly pursued, in the most glorious discoveries and eternal certainty" (*Lectures on Faith*, 24; emphasis added). Earlier in this same lecture, Paul's phrase, "feel after God," invites us to question "what it was that *stirred up the faith* of multitudes to *feel after* [God]—to search after a knowledge of his character, perfections and attributes, until they become extensively acquainted with him, and not only commune with him and behold his glory, but be partakers of his power and stand in his presence" (*Lectures on Faith*, 17–18; emphasis added). The scriptures' influence in helping us reach lies in their ability to stir up, arouse, and excite each soul to feel after, search for, and inquire into the nature of God with the assurance that our pursuit will end in glorious discoveries. When we knock, the door will open. Scriptural accounts of past generations are frequently the door knocker.

Our knocking may take the form of the prayer of counsel.

We have pondered; we have ideas; we have discerned a direction; we are now ready to counsel with the Lord. Alma taught his son Helaman to "counsel with the Lord in all thy doings, and he will direct thee for good" (Alma 37:37). Counseling suggests mutual respect coming from both sides and a recognition that what the other thinks is worthy of consideration. Certainly the Lord is far wiser than we are, but he wants us to learn to reason and think as he does. Remember, he is trying to turn us into gods. He truly is interested in what we are thinking. He will counsel *with* us, not counsel *at* us. George MacDonald grasped the spirit of the prayer of counseling as well as any Christian thinker I have read. He said: "What is the whole system of things for, but our education? Does God care for suns and planets and satellites, for divine mathematics and ordered harmonies, more than for his children? . . . He lays no plans irrespective of his children; and his design being that they shall be free, active, live things, he sees that space be kept for them: they need room to struggle out of their chrysalis, to undergo the change that comes with the waking will, and to enter upon the divine sports and labors of children in the house and domain of their Father. *Surely he may keep his plans in a measure unfixed, waiting the free desire of the individual soul!*" (MacDonald, *Unspoken Sermons*, 169; emphasis added). Counseling with the Lord, therefore, requires the free expression of our own thoughts. It is a two-way communication, not only a child listening patiently to the wisdom of a Father, even the wisest of all Fathers. He listens to us as intently as we listen to him. Our expressions to him must be given with "no apprehension that God might be displeased with him for saying what he would like, and not leaving it all to his Father. Neither [does the child] regard his Father's plans as necessarily so fixed that they could not be altered to his prayer. The true son-faith is that which comes with boldness, fearless of the Father doing anything but what is right fatherly, patient, and full of loving-kindness. . . . What stupidity of perfection would that be which left no margin about God's work, no room for change of plan upon change of fact—yea, even the mighty change that, behold now at length, his child is praying!" (ibid., 168, 170). This too is a type of knocking.

If we wish to meet God face to face, we must learn to knock and recognize in our own lives the Lord's knocking in return. We feel after him, but he also feels after us. We want to find him, but he also wants to find us. Friendship always flows in both directions. There must be two faces for face-to-face relationships. You and I are not the only ones who wish for heavenly encounters with Deity. God also desires them. There is nothing quite so dampening of a hoped-for meeting than to find that the opposite party has no wish to speak to you. The opposite is equally true—nothing is so encouraging than the knowledge that face-to-face conversations are welcomed by the other person. As regards our Father in Heaven, did he not say, "Draw near unto me and I will draw near unto you; seek me diligently and ye shall find me; ask, and ye shall receive; knock, and it shall be opened unto you"? (D&C 88:63). We usually read the oft-quoted *ask*, *seek*, and *knock* as a desire for knowledge or understanding. Light and truth will be imparted. Without question, we can read those words with this in mind. Yet the Doctrine and Covenants version of this familiar formula gives new meaning with the introductory phrase "draw near unto me." It places these well-known commands into a new context. Rather than just knowledge or doctrinal understanding, it seems it is the Lord himself—sharing those face-to-face encounters—we are seeking and finding. It is his visage we long to see when the door opens to our hopeful knockings.

RIVERS IN
DRY PLACES

*For thus sayeth the high and lofty One
that inhabiteth eternity, whose name is Holy;
I dwell in the high and holy place.*

—ISAIAH 57:15

The Most High in the High
and Holy Place

As we experience all of the reachings we've discussed, all of the feelings after God, we will learn that one leads into another. They are more closely interrelated than we may first notice. I have found in my own life a fairly consistent pattern of connectedness. I may begin with a pouring out. Almost without fail, that pouring out results in an increase in my love for God, not only for listening to my problems and sins so patiently, but for the inevitable pouring in that follows. He has allowed us to find him. I discover myself entering into the Prayer of Quiet. I begin reaching through desire. Love and desire, or feeling after and finding him, creates in my soul those virtues Teresa spoke of. My soul responds to the watering of its garden. The flowers of virtue begin to bloom, and I plead with God sometimes to show me what I can do in return. He may reveal what service or consecration would please him, but far more often a new wrestling may commence, or I begin pondering and searching for ways to become anxiously engaged in his causes. I become active in the

Lord's own prayer wherein he pleaded, "Thy kingdom come. Thy will be done in earth, as it is in heaven" (Matthew 6:10; see also Luke 11:2). Are we not in reality the agents of that kingdom's coming? In time, our familiarity grows; we know the voice on the other side of the door and are more comfortable and confident that it truly is our Lord's voice. Equally he knows ours. However, we must always beware of the error of stoicism, the belief that you can always do what you did once. More often than not, our pouring out and our wrestling, our reaching with desire and our knocking, our willingness to believe and to act will bring answers. The sister in my ward honestly wondered if our prayers will be enough. Through reaching high to the heavens, through pouring out, wrestling, believing, acting, desiring, and knocking, they will.

I once had an interesting dream, which I have pondered frequently and in which I have found many applications. Here is just one. I was walking by a dry riverbed filled with boulders. The banks were steep enough that the river could hold a great deal of water. There were many boats of various types and sizes up and down the river, each equipped with oars. As I walked along the bank, I watched people straining against the oars, trying to move their boats along the sand and rocks of the riverbed. Because there was no water, their progress was a continuous picture of frustration. Many had given up and sat holding the oars disconsolately without rowing. I was filled with a deep empathy as I watched the laboring, exhausted, or apathetic rowers.

I was given to understand that the riverbed represented

life without the living water of truth, which flows abundantly from our Father in Heaven and his Son, and that one could have as much or as little as one desired. I thought immediately of Ezekiel's vision of the rising waters he saw springing up from the doors of the temple and flowing into the dry wastes of the desert (see Ezekiel 47). This river became ever deeper as it wound its way forward. I reflected on the Savior's promise that "he that believeth on me, as the scripture hath said, out of his belly shall flow rivers of living water" (John 7:38). He also promised that he would be for us "as rivers of water in a dry place" (Isaiah 32:2) and would "open rivers in high places, and fountains in the midst of the valleys: I will make the wilderness a pool of water, and the dry land springs of water" (Isaiah 41:18). Isaiah also gave us God's assurance that he "will do a new thing. . . . [He] will even make a way in the wilderness, and rivers in the desert" (Isaiah 43:19). These rivers bring what we all long for: peace. "I will extend peace to her like a river" (Isaiah 66:12).

The Lord mourns for our plight also as he watches his children trying to progress, straining at their oars against shifting dry sand and hard rock. "O that thou hadst hearkened to my commandments—then had thy peace been as a river" (1 Nephi 20:18). I believe firmly that our Father in Heaven wants to reveal his truth and goodness and beauty to us. He does not wish us to row futilely among sand and boulders, but row powerfully among the currents of his revealed will and mercy. We must, however, desire the water fervently. Our reaching must lift high as the heavens. Do we not call our God "the Most High," and does he not dwell in "the high and holy place"? (Isaiah 57:15). May we feel after God and find him. May we know him face to face. May we reach in such a way that prayer will always be enough. May the flowing waters fill our riverbeds and deliver us safely into the ocean of our Father in Heaven's compassion, where we may enjoy face-to-face love and sharing eternally, an ocean which never ends and has no veil to reach through. There will be no "up" in that kingdom, no ceiling to pray our way through, but instead a sharing with that Being who "comprehendeth all things, and all things are before him, and all things are round about him; and he is above all things, and in all things, and is through all things, and is round about all things; and all things are by him, and of him, even God, forever and ever" (D&C 88:41).

THE BLESSING

I can conceive of no better conclusion than the beautiful blessing so beloved of the Jewish people, which was taught by the Lord himself from the Sinai wilderness. May we all know its fullest and highest fulfillment:

> *The Lord bless thee, and keep thee: The Lord make his face shine upon thee, and be gracious unto thee: The Lord lift up his countenance upon thee, and give thee peace. (Numbers 6:24–27)*

WORKS CITED

Bliss, Philip Paul. "More Holiness Give Me." *Hymns of The Church of Jesus Christ of Latter-day Saints*, no. 131. Salt Lake City: The Church of Jesus Christ of Latter-day Saints, 1985.

Brown, Hugh B. In Conference Report, October 1967, 115–21.

Browning, Robert. "La Saisiaz." In *The Agamemnon of Aeschylus: La Saisiaz [et al.]*. New York: Houghton Mifflin, 1894.

Clayton, William. "Come, Come, Ye Saints." *Hymns of The Church of Jesus Christ of Latter-day Saints*, no. 30. Salt Lake City: The Church of Jesus Christ of Latter-day Saints, 1985.

Frost, Robert. *The Poetry of Robert Frost*. Edited by Edward Connery Lathem. New York: Holt, Rinehart and Winston, 1969.

Home for Christmas. Audio CD. "I'll Be Home for Christmas." Words and music by Kim Gannon, Walter Kent, and Buck Ram. Performed by Hilary Weeks. Salt Lake City: Shadow Mountain Records, 2011.

Lectures on Faith. Salt Lake City: Deseret Book, 1985.

MacDonald, George. *Unspoken Sermons*. Charleston, SC: BiblioBazaar, 2006.

Medwick, Cathleen. *Teresa of Avila: The Progress of a Soul*. Knopf: New York, 1999.

Montgomery, James. "Prayer Is the Soul's Sincere Desire." *Hymns of The Church of Jesus Christ of Latter-day Saints*, no. 145. Salt Lake City: The Church of Jesus Christ of Latter-day Saints, 1985.

Pascal, Blaise. *Pensées and The Provincial Letters*. Translated by W. F. Trotter. New York: Modern Library, 1941.

Saint Teresa of Ávila. *The Way of Perfection*. Translated and edited by E. Allison Peers. New York: Image Books, 1964.

Thayne, Emma Lou. "Where Can I Turn for Peace?" *Hymns of The Church of Jesus Christ of Latter-day Saints*, no. 129. Salt Lake City: The Church of Jesus Christ of Latter-day Saints, 1985.

Wilcox, S. Michael. *Sunset: On the Passing of Those We Love*. Salt Lake City: Deseret Book, 2011.

———. *The Ten-Day Daughter*. Salt Lake City: Deseret Book, 2012.

INDEX